YOUR CAREER
IN PUBLIC RELATIONS

This book gives a total picture of public relations, whether for corporations, non-profit concerns and government departments, agencies, or trade associations. It clearly defines the varying nature of the work involving such media as newspapers, magazines, radio and TV. It surveys the opportunities for women as well as men; offers invaluable advice on how to obtain the proper education and how to break into the field; shows what public relations can mean in terms of challenge and reward.

YOUR CAREER
IN PUBLIC RELATIONS

This book gives a total picture of public relations, whether for corporations, non-profit concerns and government departments, agencies, or trade associations. It clearly defines the varying nature of the work involving such media as newspapers, magazines, radio and TV. It surveys the opportunities for women as well as men; offers invaluable advice on how to obtain the proper education and how to break into the field; shows what public relations can mean in terms of challenge and reward.

Jody Donohue

YOUR CAREER IN PUBLIC RELATIONS

Illustrated with photographs

Julian Messner · New York

Published simultaneously in the United States and
Canada by Julian Messner, a division of Simon &
Schuster, Inc., 1 West 39 Street, New York, N.Y.
10018. All rights reserved.

PRINTED IN THE UNITED STATES OF AMERICA
LIBRARY OF CONGRESS CATALOG CARD NO. 67–21616

For each of you—
with deepest gratitude

Contents

Contents

1 Public Relations— Just What is It?

"It's exciting to report this news today, ladies and gentlemen. Each food capsule in this packet is potent enough to keep you well fed for one week. Men in orbit have survived for months on these capsules—eating nothing else. Now we want you, the food editors of this nation, to test them. They're the same capsules the government has chosen for civilian passengers to eat on the first lunar flight next August."

The president of America's largest food processing company continued talking to the note-taking editors who had just devoured a four-course luncheon.

Two television cameras focused on the president; three network microphones picked up his message, and flash bulbs popped periodically. Newspaper and magazine food editors fingered the food concentrate packages thoughtfully; some studied their press kits, then listened harder.

Business writers from the nation's wire services and news magazines underscored their notes; this news would have a powerful effect on the stock market.

At one side of the room, company officials listened intently to their president; the public relations vice-president knew best what would come next—he had written the speech! Two of his young associates sat quietly at the table, relieved everything was going well. The press had shown up; press kits had been ready in time—complete with pictures, releases, fact sheets and product samples. On-the-spot news coverage was good. The program was moving smoothly—including the electronic mike system which had kicked up earlier.

"Good work," the public relations VP smiled at his assistants. "It's first rate."

The public relations staff exchanged glances. Praise from their boss didn't come lightly. They had done a good job— the boss knew it; they knew it.

This example of a major announcement from a big food company is typical of public relations activity going on daily throughout the country. Although food for regular lunar flights may still be food for fancy, the handling of news conferences is routine for public relations people. It's all part of the day-to-day business of the world called public relations.

Just what *is* public relations?

Public relations is the business of working with and for good will—to sell a product, an idea or a system. Public relations is a definite technique of telling what's good about a company, a product, a service—or even a country. Sometimes public relations is explaining what's not so good, too.

It's the systematic communication of ideas; it is a kind of selling, in fact.

Here's what one dictionary has to say about it:

"Public relations: the activities of an industry, unit, corporation, government, or other organization in building and maintaining sound and productive relations with special publics such as customers, employees, and the public at large, so as to adapt itself to its environment and interpret itself to society."

Men in public relations often have different definitions of their field. One of the founding fathers of PR, Edward L. Bernays, says "Public relations [is] concerned with improving relationships between an institution and the public on which it is dependent. It tries to establish a mutuality of interest, an adjustment to the public. Persuasion and information are basic to mutual understanding."

Another leader in the field, John W. Hill, founder of the world's largest public relations firm, Hill & Knowlton, comments: "I have never advised or come across a definition of 'public relations' that was satisfactory to me."

You can ask several different PR men for definitions of their business, and you'll get several different answers. One chapter of PRSA (Public Relations Society of America), the major association in the field, has published twenty-three different definitions.

Public relations is a glamour business. You work with the media—the newspaper men and women, the magazine editors and writers, with radio and television people. You work under pressures and deadlines; you also work with the humdrum daily routine of just doing a job.

Public relations is a combination of exciting assignments and the uneventful. One week you may be handling press events for the opening of a great new airport; the next week you could be preparing an employee's booklet on the care of office equipment. Some days you'll spend writing and rewriting copy, editing stories and preparing reports.

Other days, public relations is the stuff dreams are made of: a maiden voyage to Mars and you're part of the press team. (Impossible? Not in twenty years!) A breakthrough in medical research: a famous pharmaceutical company, your client, discovers a cure for cancer. Or a more mundane event: a metropolitan bank presenting its annual Christmas program to the public. This time, an underprivileged group from Appalachia is brought to the big city to sing its songs and sell its handmade products in the bank's lobby. (A bank has heart—*and* public relations!)

One fact is vitally important to remember about public relations: the story must be accurate. Facts must be true. A public relations person works with all the press—and just how many times do you think a reporter or editor would

That brings up "image building."

Public relations people are sometimes considered "image builders" because their job is to tell the story of a product, company or organization. If the result of good public relations work creates a certain concept or idea about a product or group, then perhaps an "image" has been created. *But unless the story is true, the facts accurate, the image has clay feet.* Public relations can't do the impossible—change the proverbial sow's ear into a silk purse. If a product is second-rate, or a politician dishonest, public relations activity can't whitewash the facts.

Most PR people are honest, hard-working citizens and won't represent or work with companies which are not ethical. Just as any profession has its phonies, the public relations world does have its share of charlatans, too. These are the backslappers, the brassy, big-talking operators who give the field a black eye.

One of the fields most closely allied with public relations is the newspaper business. M. L. Stein makes an observation in his book *Your Career in Journalism* that also applies to public relations:

"Most newsmen conduct themselves honestly and ethically and are respected by their sources and fellow citizens. A small minority, unfortunately, operate under their own rules; these individuals are usually second-rate reporters to begin with. The truly outstanding newspaper men and women do not have to resort to questionable practice. They have earned their reputation by skill, hard work and a sense of dedication to the principles of truth, accuracy and fair play."

Journalism is a sound training ground for public relations work. Experience in any of the media—newspapers, magazines, radio or TV—is highly desired by potential PR employers. Journalism gives you the kind of working tools that are invaluable: you become a clear, concise writer; you learn to work under pressure; you sense the news aspect of an event or situation immediately; and you know what to do about it. You'll probably type at a fair clip; mechanical skills are important in PR, too.

There are many differences between the journalist and the public relations person, because they belong to two different fields. The journalist may be a crackerjack at his craft, but his training and experience usually limit him to one specific media. In public relations, you must be able to tailor your material to newspapers or magazines, and you must know the proper format for presenting ideas to radio and TV people. The requirements for each are distinct; these differences and the proper techniques will be discussed in later chapters.

Another important difference between the journalist and public relations work is recognition. Newsmen are special in the eyes of the world; they enjoy a status and prestige that just doesn't happen to the PR worker. He's behind the scenes; his satisfactions must come from knowing his efforts have helped someone else achieve recognition. Is it important that people admire what you do? Most people don't understand what public relations is, and it's harder to admire something that's not understood. So if you're too concerned about public acclaim, you'd better think twice about public relations. On the other hand, if you're not too concerned about outside approval and like what you already know about public relations, there may be an exciting career ahead for you.

If you're creative, like working with ideas and can develop ideas into practical programs, that's another plus on your side. If you're sensitive to people, aware of moods and responses, so much the better. It's all part of being able to communicate with people.

Communication, of course, is telling someone something so he understands. This may sound simple—but have you tried to tell a friend something special, and he just doesn't "get the message"?

In public relations, communicating takes many forms. The good PR person knows how to work with all the tools available. These include:

—meetings
—booklets
—speeches
—films
—publicity

All of these tools will be discussed in chapters that explain just how you work with each, and how you can reach various "publics."

That's a word that is used often in public relations; it's a term you should make part of your vocabulary now.

A "public" is a particular group of people—society is made up of many different publics. The various publics are the concern of public relations practitioners—what the publics are, who comprises them, and how they're reached are vital to the success of public relations activity.

A pharmaceutical firm making tranquilizers, for example, wants to reach doctors who might recommend the tablets. The French champagne producers want to explain their product to social leaders and upper-income society; a stereo-component maker wants his message to reach hi-fi and electronic buffs. A yarn producer wants to influence knitters.

A farm equipment firm has a definite public or audience

for news and facts about its products, and the PR person who advised the firm to "talk" to apartment dwellers wouldn't be doing much of a job—much less reaching the proper public for his company or client. Every company, organization or government has some effect on a particular public or group of publics; your job is to know what specific publics will be affected by the actions of your company or organization.

What results do you want? Good will—that's the business of public relations; good will opens the door to understanding and acceptance—for an idea, service or a product. Acceptance by a public or publics is the desired goal for a company making missile parts, a charity group, a university or maybe a man from Massachusetts who wants to be President.

Jobs in PR are within two major categories: either corporations—companies or organizations—or public relations agencies, where you work with clients.

There are job positives on either side of the picture: the corporate or company job is more secure and has less pressure than an agency job. But it's apt to be less exciting, because you're always dealing with the same company.

A PR agency offers greater variety and stimulation, primarily because clients change and you work on different problems and projects. A later chapter explores the possibilities of each area.

Today more than fifty thousand people in the United States and Canada earn a good living working at various levels of public relations. If you enjoy being where the action is, working closely with a company's top management, and touching the pulse of people—public relations is for you.

2 What's in It for Me?

PUBLIC RELATIONS OPPORTUNITY

A challenging opportunity in Public Relations has been created by Trent University in Peterborough. The holder of this position will report to the President, with responsibilities for a broad and varied program of news and feature assignments, the arrangement of speeches, the publication of reports and the production of print, radio and T.V. copy. He will also have certain responsibilities in regard to planning and arranging some University functions and public occasions, and in the area of community relations.

The successful applicant will be a university graduate, preferably with experience in journalism and writing, public and cultural affairs and/or public relations. He should be in the age range of 25 to 40. Applications from younger university graduates with interests in these fields will be welcomed as well as applications from persons with greater experience. He should have a personal interest in university and related affairs, and the ability to work creatively with academic and administrative colleagues on the staff of a new and developing institution with a distinctive character and educational philosophy. Salary will be fully commensurate with background and experience.

This ad appeared in the November 12, 1965, issue of the Toronto *Globe & Mail*, and it is quoted to show you the opportunities that are available in public relations. Ads like this—though not always so explicit—are running in major daily papers in every metropolitan area of the country. Look through the classified ads of the big-city daily newspaper in your area, and you'll see listings in the "Help Wanted" sections for PR people. For example, on the first Sunday in 1966, The New York *Times* listed more than fifty openings for men and nearly two dozen for women in public relations. A rundown of "Help Wanted-Male" ads reads like this:

PUBLIC RELATIONS TRNE $6900
deg in Eng or Journalism major corp

PUBLIC Relations (interesting field), features and releases—weekly newsletter. Newspaper bkgrd. $7-7500

P/R Jr—top grad—2 yrs exp—fee neg. Top ind'l corp in N.Y. $8500

PR PROFESSIONAL
Blue-chip public relations agency seeks mature, intelligent man who can imaginatively combine sound counseling experience with highly-active staff services. Financial PR helpful. Salary commensurate with quality of candidate.

PUB REL Junior Writer $7000 Giant midtown industrial corp. Now writing for newspaper or company

PUB REL SPEECH WRITER, to $15,000 Strong

feeling, liberal area—bkgd sociology/economics
5 yrs. co. feature exp-deg

PUBLICITY. Art Shows, Entertainment. $125

On the same day in the "Help Wanted-Female" columns,
the listings included these:

PUBLIC RELATIONS
Exp. working with volunteers & good writing abilities. Excellent oppty for expd, capable person with
dynamic social agency. Salary commensurate.

PR SECRETARY
For leading agency, top skills, judgment—eager to
learn, college graduate. $100

PUB REL—Fashion writing exp. $7,500

PUBLICITY ASST/GAL FRI   TO $115
This is an excellent spot for a coll grad or some
coll with min 6 mos exp in publicity. Lots of press
contact so must know how to place a release. Opty
to write press release as well. Typing 45.

Good jobs in public relations are available in major metropolitan areas throughout the country. Opportunities in PR
are there right now—and they're growing at a remarkably
fast pace. Within the next ten years, the opportunities for
jobs in public relations will increase more than 100 percent,
and today there are more openings than there are qualified
young people to fill them.

Let's review the specifics of the first ad quoted, the "Public
Relations Opportunity," because the requirements and qualifications are the most explicit. The journalist's "five W" technique should reveal all that's important to know—who,
what, when, where and why.

Who is the ad for? A young man or woman with the proper qualifications. In this particular ad for a PR person, the requisites are clear-cut. In the other ads, specific requirements are not spelled out but you can be sure both the job and qualifications are clear in the employer's mind!

The first requisite listed is that the "successful applicant will be a university graduate." If you're seriously interested in public relations, you'll be better off with college training. Most of the young people being hired today are college graduates or have had some college or university training. In the past ten years, the importance of a good, solid academic background has become increasingly important for young applicants going after PR jobs.

There's no rule about education and public relations, of course. You certainly can get into the field and may do very well without a college degree—but it will be harder to get your first job. Your boss, for example, might not have a degree; indeed, he might not have had any college at all. But he is a couple of generations ahead of you, and the situation has changed. Given two young applicants for the same PR job, one with college and one without it, the employer generally will favor the college graduate.

Public relations is not a recognized profession such as medicine or law; there's no shingle or parchment you can frame and hang in your office to prove you've had the necessary schooling and training. In fact, as far as PR is concerned, college is something like money—you may not have much, but some sure helps!

If you are truly serious and ambitious about your future in public relations and have a choice now whether to go on to school or not, there's only one sound decision: go to college. The kinds of academic training that will be most helpful to you, as well as schools which offer courses in public relations, are discussed in a later chapter.

What is a "Public Relations Opportunity"? The ad offers a

challenge to someone interested in education and a university environment. You may be intrigued by other areas—industry, commerce, government or perhaps the world of entertainment, rather than education. Regardless of which general area you find most appealing, there is one consistent qualification for a public relations person, and it is mentioned specifically in the ad: ". . . the ability to work creatively . . ."

Are you creative? Can you originate ideas, then carry them through to a productive conclusion? Say the twenty-fifth anniversary of your dramatic club is coming up next semester; would you have ideas for "celebrating" or commemorating the occasion? *Workable* ideas that would reflect favorably on the club and give it a boost in the eyes of the school and the community? Would you think, for instance, to invite the really successful graduates now in television and theatre to address the present club members? Would you invite your principal, the deans, everyone important in school, as well as certain local citizens—maybe the mayor? Would you have ideas to set up an outstanding program highlighting the anniversary? If so, you're a creative thinker.

Creativity works in a number of ways, of course, but creative people share certain characteristics. Here's what a leading scientist observed about this vital public relations qualification—creativity:

"Creative people are especially observant, and they value accurate observation (telling themselves the truth) more than other people do. They see things as others do, but also as others do not.

"They are born with greater brain capacity: they have the ability to hold many ideas at once, and to compare more ideas with one another—hence to make a richer synthesis.

"They are by constitution vigorous, and have available to them an exceptional fund of psychic and physical energy.

"Their universe is thus more complex, and in addition they usually lead more complex lives."

Does this sound like you? Good! You're on the right track, because creativity is a function of the effective public relations person.

When is this opportunity? Right now. And right into to-morrow. The possibilities for carving out a career in public relations couldn't be better. Growth of the number of people in the field is remarkable—and still on a strong upsurge. In 1950, the U.S. Census Bureau reported 19,000 public relations workers and publicity writers. Ten years later, the total had *jumped 64 percent*—to more than 31,000. In the five years from 1960 to 1965, the U.S. Census Bureau estimates an increase to 60,000. The Public Relations Publishing Company reports that more than 57,000 people worked in public relations in 1965. So the opportunities are increasing. As our population expands, so does the need for better communication and understanding. By 1980, experts predict that 200,-000 men and women will be working in the ranks of public relations practitioners. You can be among those counted.

Where is PR activity going on? The ad searching for a competent PR applicant for university PR work wanted someone in Peterborough, a small city near Toronto. This is, however, an exception to the general pattern in public relations, which is primarily a big-city business. Most of the jobs are in metropolitan areas. Cities are the communications centers, and using the various communication facilities effectively is basic to public relations activity.

So another requisite for your success in PR is city living; within twenty years, the majority of America's 250 million people will be clustered in a few sprawling great city areas. The problems that will result from this concentration of population *and* industry will create tremendous needs for good public relations. Industry will be producing at incredible speed; automation will have moved into high gear; communications will have an international scope of storybook force.

The trend is clear toward urban living. The Futurama exhibit at the New York World's Fair some years ago suggested a wonder-world of great cities stacked like miracle high-rise apartments, roads and throughways intertwining below a giant metropolis. Airports atop buildings; industry booming deep in caverns and underwater near the twinkling magic cities. Millions of people thronged together, working efficiently and effectively. Public relations will play an important part in making this a reality, because survival will depend more strongly on effective communications and real understanding.

Geographically, most jobs will be in the cities, but where does public relations function in our society? Here are a few areas, in no order of importance:

INDUSTRY AND COMMERCE.   As population swings toward metropolitan centers, the problems of industry will increase. Industry must sell its products to survive, and the concentration of the people or publics who are affected by any given industry's products must be influenced favorably. As men and machines move into more compact quarters, problems arise. Public relations plays an increasingly important role in solving problems and moving merchandise—whether it's heavy industrial equipment or next season's fashions.

TOURISM.   As any country progresses economically, the level of affluence rises. People have more money to spend. Internationalism becomes much more important. Foreign lands are closer; exploring of the unknown becomes a very real possibility. Public relations already is important in the international exchange of peoples and products; in to-

morrow's world, traveling to all parts of the world
will be usual traffic. PR at all levels—from government policies down to attracting tourists to buy
tickets—is active business.

GOVERNMENT. The role of public relations in government is important. This vital area will be discussed in detail in a later chapter; this is an open
and challenging area for young people interested
in both public relations and the remarkable ma-
chinery of government.

POLITICS. This field is akin to government, of
course, but definitely demands a different brand of
public relations activity. Politicians of every level
and caliber depend on competent PR counsel
throughout their political life. Franklin Roosevelt
and John Kennedy were masters of the techniques
of public relations. (An early genius in PR activity, Louis B. Howe, was an advisor to President
Roosevelt.) Presidential press secretaries have become national figures as a consequence of their
jobs. Both national and local political candidates
rely on PR advisors to know the pulse of public
opinion. (Not always too happily!) This special
area also will be explored in depth in another chapter.

Several other major areas require the talents of public relations people—including the non-profit service organizations, such as hospitals, youth groups, charity and health
organizations. You may find a rewarding role as public relations advisor to one of these worthy groups.

Still another vital area offering great potential to public
relations hopefuls is trade associations. These are groups of
competitive business people joined together to serve their
membership and the public. Today more than thirteen thou-

sand such associations exist, and more than two thousand of these associations are national. The very nature of trade organizations implies public relations activity—communicating the organization's needs and problems internally and explaining its functions to the various external publics. There's a great future in this area—for the number of associations will explode as the population expands.

If you're intrigued by the field, let's answer the final question of "why"—the fifth of our journalistic five W's.

Why go into public relations? The answer should be obvious—because you're interested! It's a lively, challenging business—one that's sure to grow in the balance of this century. Business, in the world of tomorrow, will find it hard going without sound PR activity.

"What's in it for me?" A living salary at the beginning and the chance to make good money in the future.

Your first job in public relations will pay about $100 a week. It might be $85 a week initially—depending on whether you're getting background experience in business or starting out as a copy boy or girl on a newspaper. If you're lucky enough to land a job in the field itself—a rarity, but becoming more common—you could start at about $125. This will continue for about a year or two.

Then you should be on your way: within five years, a hardworking public relations junior (and you're still a junior for the first decade) can work himself up to $7,500—maybe $8,000. By the time you've been working in corporate PR or a public relations firm for ten years, you should be earning at least $10,000.

The top men—and a few women—command outstanding salaries. A recent survey by the American University's School of Business Administration reveals that among 250 corporations, the average salary for PR Director was $31,-642. According to this study, 14 percent of the PR men made between $10,000 and $20,000; 13 percent made between

$20,000 and $25,000, 9 percent between $25,000 and $30,-
000—and right up the line to the 2 percent of the total companies queried which paid their top PR men at least $70,000
a year. So there's gold in them thar hills . . . but it takes
some digging to get at it!

You can earn a comfortable living in public relations, and
a satisfying one. There's even some indication you can get
rich in the business—but there's no "get rich quick" formula
in PR. It's a long, occasionally difficult road, but well worth
the effort.

3 How It All Started

The first young man or woman ever to have a "beginning
job" in public relations might have been employed to mingle
with the Athenians who thronged the Agora some five centuries before Christ. The assignment would have been, "Keep
your ears open and tell us what the citizens are saying to one
another about the problems of the day and how the government is handling them." Even the rulers of Ancient Greece
tried to put a finger on the pulse of public opinion!

Other evidence of early public relations activity is found
in the history of the Roman Empire. Emperor Augustus Cae-
sar gave his friend and advisor Gaius Maecenes two specific
public relations assignments. One was to keep abreast of
public opinion and inform the "blunter intelligence" of government about what Roman citizens were thinking. The
other job given Maecenes was to help "create opinion for his
day and all time." Much of our present knowledge and opinion about ancient Rome can be traced to Maecenes' influence
on the writings of Horace and Virgil. Consider *Georgics*, for
example, an effort to encourage city dwellers to move to the
country to work on farms and produce food for the growing

population. It was also a Roman who coined the phrase that still rings today not only in public relations but also in all democratic nations, "The voice of the people is the voice of God."

Many early Roman poets and balladeers were paid by those they glorified in verse and song. This was why in his *Republic* Plato condemned poets as "special pleaders"; he urged they all be suppressed except those employed by the state to promote its own welfare—a suggestion not unlike that made occasionally even in modern times.

Other public relations beginnings can be traced in all early civilizations. Kings of Ancient India employed spies who, besides carrying on ordinary espionage activities, also kept the king posted on public opinion. In England, the early kings designated a chancellor as "keeper of the King's conscience," who served as communications intermediary between government and the people. The word "propaganda" has its origin in the Catholic Church's College for the Propagation of the Faith.

Historians chronicling the story of our own country are agreed that the American Revolution was no spontaneous uprising. Actually, few public movements of any kind are spontaneous. They require leadership, a voice, and generally much patient planning. The American Revolution was the product of the work of a few who had, among other qualities, some sense of public relations. The Declaration of Independence itself speaks of "a decent respect to the opinions of mankind." Samuel Adams, Benjamin Franklin, Thomas Paine and Alexander Hamilton were among our pioneers in public relations as well as fathers of our country.

In his monograph published by the Foundation for Public Relations Research and Education, Allen Nevins describes the Federalist Papers as "history's finest public relations job." Other historians may dispute the importance of the role the Papers played in winning ratification of the Constitution. But with mass media then far less developed than today, it probably is no exaggeration to say that the Constitution would have failed ratification had not the Federalist Papers persuasively carried the argument throughout the territory. Nevins describes it as "essentially a public relations exercise," crediting Hamilton, James Madison and John Jay with "keen public relations instincts."

However, public relations, as it generally is practiced today, and the kind of activity you will do, had its real beginnings around 1900. What went before was public relations, of course, but as a specialized field of activity adhering to fairly standard methods of analysis and procedure, the emergence began with the twentieth century. Cutlip and Center, in their text *Effective Public Relations,* divide the era from 1900 to the present into five segments.

First is the period 1900 to 1917, the "muckraking years." Second is the World War I period of 1917-1919. The third begins in 1919 and runs until 1933, the beginning of the New Deal. The fourth, 1933-1945, includes the Depression and World War II. And finally, the last is from 1945 to the present.

This is neither a text nor a history book, however, so only a few of the important moments will be noted. If you're considering a public relations career, you will find it helpful to understand that you follow in the steps of some extraordinarily able men and women. Some insights into public relations history will also help you gain perspective and understand that public relations is not just someone's "bright idea," but an outgrowth of historical forces that have shaped our nation and our lives.

At the turn of the century, two of these forces began to nourish the growth of modern public relations. The first was the onslaught of the muckrakers. "Muckraker" was a term generally applied to journalists whose stinging prose dramatized the economic and social excesses of which the business

community was at least partly guilty at that time. Ida Tar-
bell, Lincoln Steffens, and Upton Sinclair, columnists with
needle-pointed pens, were among the most notable muckrakers. They were not always fair or accurate, but they were
dramatic. The business leaders of the day, behind their customary cloak of secrecy were stunned, hurt and helpless.
They had neither the wish nor the talent to respond. Not
until it was almost too late did they have any notion of the
mortal danger they faced from rising public clamor. In
short, business leaders had not yet learned that public opinion really does matter.

As always happens under such circumstances, politicians
go where the votes are. Political leaders of the day, notably
Theodore Roosevelt, Robert LaFollette and Woodrow Wilson,
provided the leadership for what became a popular reform
movement to curb the power of big business.

The lesson for public relations people is that business was
found guilty before the bar of public opinion without ever
presenting its defense. It was something like being hauled
off to prison without even knowing that a police force and a
court existed. It may not have been an injustice, but it certainly was a surprise to the business community.

And so, cast in the unhappy role of the "bad guys" of the
time, business began to seek out those who might help win
them a parole. They found men like Ivy Lee, Theodore Vail,
J. Hampton Baumgartner and James Ellsworth, each of
whom made an important contribution to building the foundation of public relations careers.

The second major turn-of-the-century force at work was
the growth of the nation's mass media. National magazines,
wire services and major metropolitan daily newspapers were
demonstrating exceptional skill in expressing and solidifying
public opinion, if not in actually forming it. For example,
McClure's Magazine was one of the big guns in the muckraker's attack. It became increasingly apparent that anyone

wishing to reach the American public, and particularly the more thoughtful citizenry, would need to establish some rapport with the media. This, too, was a brand new idea to the business community who generally regarded any query from a journalist as an impertinent invasion of privacy.

Initially, businessmen thought they could win favorable editorial treatment in the media by withholding or granting the advertising dollar. In some instances this worked, as it still does occasionally today. But to the publisher with principle and good sense who knew that his own success depended upon the editorial independence of his publication, flexing the advertising muscle served only as a red flag. The publication beholden to its advertisers instead of its readers quickly ceases to serve either.

The only alternative, then, was to turn to those who knew something about the editorial interests of the media and could constructively serve both the publications and those who had a story to tell. This accounts for the fact that almost the entire first generation of public relations people came from the editorial staffs of newspapers and magazines.

Ivy Ledbetter Lee is often identified as the founder of modern public relations. This is arguable, but there is little doubt that his contribution was unequaled by any of the other early practitioners. First, he operated in an open and forthright manner with no attempt to deceive either the news media or his clients. Before Lee entered the business, it was customary for a public relations firm or press agent to conceal the identity of his client. Also, it was usual for the client to hide the fact it had hired a press agent. This undercover operation attempted to slant the news or suppress unfavorable news without acknowledging the source. The Publicity Bureau, one of the early firms, for example, represented the railroads. But it operated in such a way that it never revealed its client. Other press agents of the period tended to follow these devious ways, interested either in building up or in suppressing news.

This character of press agentry made Lee's classic "Declaration of Principles" a truly startling advance. His Declaration was sent to a long list of editors when Lee undertook representation of the anthracite coal operators engaged in a bitter labor dispute. His Declaration is so simple and succinct a statement of policy that it has not been improved even to this day. It said, in part: "This is not a secret press bureau. All our work is done in the open. We aim to supply news. This is not an advertising agency; if you think any of our matter ought properly to go to your business office, do not use it. Our matter is accurate. In brief, our plan is, frankly and openly, on behalf of business concerns and public institutions, to supply the press and the public of the United States prompt and accurate information concerning subjects which it is of value and interest to the public to know about."

With those few words, Lee pointed the direction for all who were to follow and made craftsmen out of men who might otherwise have been mere favor seekers.

Lee's second major contribution to public relations is the advice he is reported to have given John D. Rockefeller, Jr. "Tell the truth," Lee advised, "because sooner or later the public will find it out anyway. And if the public doesn't like what you are doing, change your policies and bring them into line with what the people want."

Just as his Declaration remains the cornerstone for public relations people in dealing with news media, this advice remains today as the cornerstone for public relations people in dealing with their clients and their employers. Good public relations must begin with good behavior. Ivy Lee was the first to make that principle stick with his clients.

This doesn't mean an institution is run by taking an opinion poll before deciding what to do. But it does mean that one running an institution must remember that the power of public opinion is the greatest of all powers in a democracy, and if practices or policies lie across the path of the public interest, they must change.

Imagine what a revolutionary concept this was to the business leaders of the first decade of this century! Yet again and again, Lee succeeded in persuading his clients to alter practices that aroused public disfavor. Public relations people can be proud of a pioneer who was truly a giant.

Wars always step up the pace of scientific and technical development. The hot crucible of national survival produces syntheses in months that might normally require years or decades. World Wars I and II had a somewhat similar effect upon the development of public relations.

Cutlip and Center observe that before World War I public relations had been primarily a defensive undertaking. It became a constructive, offensive force in the war with the advent of George Creel's Committee on Public Information. The Committee's principal mission was to plan and conduct the Liberty Loan drives to sell war bonds to the American public. It performed this task superbly in five successive campaigns during the war years. Creel, himself a journalist, recruited to the Committee the nation's finest communications specialists from journalism, advertising, education and the infant public relations business. Working under wartime conditions with such a talented and diverse group gave the public relations contingent a great training opportunity. Creel's "college" trained the practitioners who advanced the frontiers of public relations rapidly in the postwar years.

In somewhat the same way, though less significantly, Elmer Davis' Office of War Information and the military information services were the schools out of which many of the post-World War II practitioners graduated.

Even the Great Depression of the early 1930s had its effect

on the development of public relations. It was described best by Earl Newsome, one of the nation's most successful and respected counselors, in a talk he made in Boston in 1963. He said, "With the great depression came the realization that 'public opinion' in this country would never again merely involve *other* people—people to be persuaded to buy our products, people to be 'educated' to accept our own estimates of ourselves. *We* also became part of 'the public,' and every individual, every corporate enterprise, and every social and political institution began to face up to the obligation to serve the progressive public interest—not necessarily as they saw it, but as most people might see it."

The muckraking days had taught the lesson that in a democracy no institution can live wrapped in secrecy. They taught that people are going to believe in institutions that serve them and whose products they use. The public's opinions will be based either on information or misinformation, but they will have opinions. No institution lives in a vacuum.

The depression days taught the second lesson: it's not enough to inform the public. It's necessary to listen as well as talk. It is not a case of "we" and "they." Everyone is in this together, and the private and public interests must always be reconciled.

Developments since World War II have been rapid and significant. They have been amply recorded in public relations literature and need not be detailed here. They include, of course, the formation of various public relations organizations culminating, through mergers, in a single national group, The Public Relations Society of America. Efforts of the PRSA include establishment of a code of public relations ethics and an accreditation program leading to accredited status for those members who demonstrate mastery of a specified body of knowledge.

Public relations has been plagued from its earliest days with opportunitsts, mediocrities, and downright dishonest

persons entering the field. There were no entrance requirements. All anyone needed was a "shingle" to "hang out." The
shabbiness of their work and the unsatisfactory results they
have achieved for their employers have made the road rough
for the man or woman serious about a public relations career.

The principal efforts in recent years of both PRSA and individual practitioners have been, on the one hand, to identify
the charlatan and, on the other, to improve the skills of the
serious worker. But a great deal remains yet to be done.

Now to step back a moment and take a long look at this
history to see what message it has for you who may enter
this field. What does the sweep of history indicate about the
real nature of the activity called public relations?

It is fairly clear. Public relations came into practice only
after mankind achieved a civilized state. There is no record
of any public relations activity among the cavemen, the
primitive jungle tribes, or even among the American Indian
tribes. The reason is that in a tribal society there are no conflicting loyalties. Loyalty to a single tribe is all that is required. There is nothing to evaluate, weigh or understand.
The tribal chief makes all the decisions—whom the individual will marry, what work he will do, how he will worship,
and often, even how he will die. The tribe is the entire world.
All that counts is what the chief decides.

In a civilized society such as ours, and even in the ancient
civilizations, an individual is a member of many tribes or
groups. For example, you are probably a member of a
church group, a club, a school student body, a political
party, and your father may be both a stockholder and a
union member. Not only do all these groups overlap, but
they frequently set up conflicting loyalties. Your church's
views may differ from those of your political party. And, of
course, your school may not fully endorse your club's views.

A society like ours is enormously complex, with groups
that conflict and overlap but also depend upon one another.

A union and a company are often in conflict, yet each is fully dependent upon the other. There is need for communication —not only in an effort to reach understanding or compromise but also in an effort to persuade. That's what public relations is all about. Public relations work arises from the need of a complex society to maintain its balance. It seeks to achieve understanding among groups in our society, and understanding is essential to survival.

Public relations didn't just happen—it didn't just appear without cause or purpose. Forces in our society created the need for it, and these forces are the healthy product of free speech and free inquiry.

Remember, there's a lot of public relations precedence behind you—and an even greater future ahead.

4 The Publics— Where PR Goes to Work

Primary concerns of every public relations man are the publics—yes, publics is correct! Every company, organization or association has its own particular publics—groups of people who are involved with that company or organization, for one reason or another. The involvement ranges from a consumer who buys a product to a stockholder who buys a share of stock.

You are part of a particular public; as a student, you automatically are part of that generic group of young people in school. If you also work, then you're part of an employee group—and since you shop, you're a consumer and part of that public. So actually, you're part of several *publics*.

If you were looking at a major television network one evening a while ago, you heard the low, vibrant notes of a familiar ballad fade softly; you watched a famous entertainer stand silhouetted in a spotlight that dimmed out of focus as the song ended. You saw the TV screen darken momentarily, then Frank Sinatra's easy, familiar grin welcomed the viewer to hear more about the life of popular music's "Chairman of the Board."

"What do you owe your public?" the interviewer asked him.

Sinatra cocked his head, his forehead wrinkled, then he replied, "You owe your public a good show. A good performance. You have a real responsibility to put on a good show." Everyone in any kind of business, whether it's selling songs or shoes, owes the public "a good show," and this includes good communication with a particular public or publics.

There are many reasons why we hold the beliefs, opinions and attitudes that we do. Reasons include our background, experiences, education and cultural exposures. All play a big part in our thinking and in our emotional patterns. *What* we think—our attitudes and opinions—creates the kind of person we are and accordingly puts us into the various classifications of publics.

What does all this have to do with public relations? Everything. It's what separates the men from the boys in the programming and execution of good public relations. It's the job of an effective, sound PR executive to decide which public all kinds of people belong to; to determine the most important public or publics for a company or client to reach; and to plan how to communicate with each effectively.

Basically, all major organizations or large firms have certain characteristics and operating areas in common. For example, every firm has suppliers from whom materials for production are bought; every company has people working in various departments; most firms sell their output to someone—directly to a consumer, to an in-between agent, or to a government. Every company or organization operates within a specific area or areas—in a specific community or a number of different communities. And most of the larger firms are listed on an exchange, which means that stockholders and the financial world are interested or involved in procedures. Each of these areas of operation involves a particular public. So regardless of what the products of a company may be—automobiles, baby food or missile parts—each has several general publics that respond to special approaches and appeals.

Ideally, public relations activity is directed toward each of the following, with emphasis on any particular aspect dictated by the special needs of the company or client:

—Employee relations
—Community relations
—Investor or stockholder relations
—Customer relations
—Sales and marketing (product publicity)
—Other specialized audiences or publics, such as professional groups, ethnic groups, special interest groups, etc.

What does "ideally" mean? Simply that public relations is still young in its development throughout the world. In your lifetime you may work with some managements that recognize the value of effective PR in all its endeavors. But you'll probably work with other managements who must be convinced that every dollar expended on public relations is a sound investment for the company, so instead of doing a total PR program, you will concentrate on one or two areas.

Now, let's consider each aspect of public relations activity. These areas are not discussed in any particular order of importance; rather, they're reviewed for their potential value to any given company's public relations programming.

Employee relations. Are you working? Then you know something about this vital area already. It covers a vast scope of activity. Entire departments often are involved with employee relations. Good employee relations is usually a matter of good communications. Does the boss care anything at all about the man working in the plant? He probably cares enough to want to keep him, but how does the man on Machine #10 know it? The boss tells him—not directly, but through every conceivable means that public relations knows how to use!

Most big companies have an employee publication. If it's interestingly presented and properly handled, the employees will read it. (You may start your job in public relations by editing a house organ.)

Management letters are another important form of business communications. When the boss wants to tell his people something, he puts it in writing for them—getting the message across, not talking down, yet maintaining a tone and manner of top management.

Employee manuals tell what the firm and job are about. If the job is handled properly, both new employees and the old-timers will read the booklet because it's all about *their* company. If it's up to you to write or rewrite the employees' manual, here are some good tips from the master of plain talk, Rudolph Flesch: "Be sure to write in the 'you' or cookbook style. Start with what they're supposed to do. Don't start with the history of the company; put that way, way back." In other words, he's saying, be brief.

Other employee communications areas that reflect the touches of good public relations activity include company movies, local publicity involving company personnel, various events for company people—open house, organized activity such as sports and intra-company competition and entertainment.

Everyone wants to "belong." No matter what we do, we all want to feel part of the first team—to be needed and necessary. The public relations man or woman who understands this need and can create communication materials that foster the feeling of belonging is a valuable addition to management.

Community relations. The relationship between a business and its community is another extremely important consideration for public relations programming and activity.

Community relations are very much like public relations itself; every company or firm has them—whether they like them or not! When a company or firm does nothing about its community relations, it's actually doing something, but by default. Therefore the results are likely to be negative.

For example, every business or company is somewhere; the main office may be in one place, branch offices may be in all the fifty states. Or perhaps only six different offices, plants or stores are scattered throughout the country. But each operation functions in a specific community, and the rapport that operation has with its own community can spell a powerful difference on the profit sheet. Good community relations indicate a lot about any company; they're a key to the overall public relations thinking. A company that works at good community relations cares about the local people.

Today, many progressive companies are deeply involved in community projects, for the simple reason that when a community prospers, so does the company. The man directing a local community project for his company isn't motivated solely by the potential profit to his firm; he's doubtless a fine human being, interested in the success of his company, his own growth and the positive position of his community. All these factors work together for a really successful combination—of people, business and community.

Let's see specifically what we're talking about. One of the most effective community relations programs recently was conducted by Columbia Gas, which supplies gas service to homes and industry throughout Pennsylvania. The firm was constantly threatened by various municipalities proposing take-over of gas service by referendum and was challenged by competitors—coal, electric and oil interests vying for community attention and dollars.

Columbia Gas created a special community goodwill program, designed to increase the status of the company's public relations directors in each of the communities serviced by the firm. By elevating the status of the men, the company reasoned, Columbia Gas itself would benefit in every local community.

The program worked, and briefly, here's how: the company decided to take advantage of our "cultural explosion"— the tremendous interest in cultural activity today—by sponsoring an important symphony orchestra concert in each of the company's gas-serviced communities. The company did not make any profit from the project; rather, various community organizations were enlisted to sell tickets for the concerts, and these respective groups shared the proceeds with the orchestra itself.

The orchestra? The Pittsburgh Symphony Orchestra. Through these community concerts, the Symphony appeared fifty-five times in various local areas, before more than seventy-five thousand local people. Service organizations promoting ticket sales divided more than $155,000.

Symphony concerts are a far cry from gas heat and cooking—but residents in all fifty-five Pennsylvania communities who enjoyed the Pittsburgh Symphony concerts may be warmer next winter for the remembering—as they flick on their gas heat thermostats.

The project required careful planning and execution from top management right down to preparation of press kits for each of the communities involved. But the goodwill engendered by this kind of activity reflects the importance of building good local community relations as a part of careful public relations programming.

Customer relations. Satisfied customers are basic to any business. It takes a lot of promotion and advertising money to get an angry customer back to buy again. He must be cajoled and courted. So the best method, of course, is to be sure he doesn't get angry in the first place.

Part of public relations encompasses the area of customer relations. As in employee relations, there is great scope and breadth to this "department," often requiring major staffing just to handle this area. Public relations is properly involved with customer relations—usually the director of public relations oversees this particular activity.

One specific covered by customer relations is research— discovering what the customer wants, then applying results to company policy. For instance, when the world's largest flowers-by-wire organization, Florists' Transworld Delivery, discovered that customers wanted to know what kind of flowers would be delivered, FTD came up with a booklet showing various kinds of floral arrangements that could be ordered in one part of the country and delivered in another. Sales skyrocketed!

Another approach to improved customer relations is used by the New York Telephone Company: each month, along with the statement, a customer receives a smart, snappy little leaflet filled with tips and ideas for homemakers. The suggestions range from easy and unusual recipes (from phone subscribers) to reminders on how to dial directly across country. It's a clever way for management to get its message over to the millions of customers in the New York City area—the phone company *does* care about every one of its subscribers.

Still another concern of the customer relations department is customer complaint letters. Often letters received from irate customers are illogical and silly, but the respondent must answer the customer courteously, accurately and as quickly as possible.

One of the country's oldest producers of yarns for hand knitting finds a new knitting "authority" every month! Consistently there's an angry knitter who writes to Bernat, complaining that the "directions are all wrong." At first the letters were turned over to the department that wrote the original instructions. Often the answer to a customer's letter sounded like a reprimand to the knitter and even implied she wasn't too bright or that she could follow the instructions without any trouble.

You know what happened? Angry customers became infuriated, refused to use Bernat yarns and talked at length to their friends about the situation. Today, a skilled technician replies to customer complaints, under the direction of the company's public relations department.

Every company that makes products for consumers will have some degree of dissatisfaction; it's human nature—and human error. But proper handling of these customers usually will soothe flustered feathers and result in an improved attitude toward the company.

Investor or stockholder relations. This public obviously is an important one for any listed company, and it's a highly heterogeneous public. During the past twenty years, the ownership of America's corporations has changed from a handful of families to millions of small investors. People from all walks of life hold stock today and more than half are women!

One of the basic tools for reaching the investor public is the annual report. This financial resumé must report financial results and present management's story in simple clear language, because the average stockholder today has little or no training in accounting or finance. But he *does* want to know what's going on in the company of which he owns a part.

Other public relations activity is directed to that segment of the investing public which does *not* hold stock in a company but might be potential shareholders. Here, the entire financial community is a concern—bankers, brokers, security analysts, investment advisors—any person or group who influences the purchase or sale of securities.

If you're involved in financial public relations, your work

also will cover these areas: stockholder letters, annual meetings, newsletters, shareholder surveys, booklets and working with the financial press.

This is an age of specialization, and if you're fascinated by the world of finance, the workings of the market, the factors which influence trading, you may well find the world of financial public relations rewarding. In a later chapter, this highly specialized aspect of PR will be explored in depth.

If you have trouble balancing your checkbook, however, you might fare better in another aspect of public relations, such as PR involved in selling.

Sales and marketing. The role of public relations as a sales tool is a growing one. More progressive managements recognize the value of utilizing the many techniques of PR in their selling program. First, product publicity helps sell, and second, the sales force must know just what management is doing to back its efforts. This serves as a stimulant to the men to sell even harder. How do they learn? You tell them—with every possible PR tool: presentations at sales meetings; regular company newsletters directed to the salesmen; reports on publicity results are just a few of the PR techniques used to support sales efforts.

One of the challenges in public relations today is the creation of unusual, effective methods to reach and persuade a particular public. This is a growing problem, one that will become even more pronounced in the years ahead when you'll be moving into the ranks of PR. As our society becomes more specialized and centralized, the need for effective communication techniques will become even more exacting. Your job—reaching a particular public within a highly concentrated area—will be difficult and will require keen creative skills.

Here's one example of public relations thinking directed toward a specific public and directly tied into a selling program. The suburban areas of any metropolitan city are sites of building booms today and will continue to be for some years ahead. Builders of a housing project in Hazlet, New Jersey, offer buyers of homes in their 500-unit project in Raritan Valley a "Move-In Kit." Called a "comprehensive resident orientation program," the package was prepared for the builders who felt their "obligations transcend merely constructing and delivering a house."

Whatever their motives, the builders offer potential buyers the direction and advice a new home-owner might need or want to know. This is indeed effective creative thinking directed to a particular audience or public, and directly coordinated with selling efforts.

Here's what a family who bought a house at Raritan Valley received: a move-in kit, sent to his old address before he moved. This included such items as labels to tell the mover where each carton and barrel should go in the new home, a master checklist of things to do before moving, a directory to the new area, tips on how to pack, even suggestions on how to prepare youngsters psychologically for moving into a new home. Then at the closing, the buyer received a thirty-three-page "Homeowners Manual" filled with home-helps and repair ideas of every description.

A successful project? The builders report they plan to adapt it for another 500-home community they're building in another area of New Jersey.

In addition to the excellent community relations a project like this engenders, there's direct publicity potential, as well. Local papers would be interested in this kind of news, and *The New York Times* ran a feature story in its real estate section on Sunday, January 30, 1966.

Specialized publics. The publics we've discussed are major categories for public relations activity for nearly every business. All of these vital areas—employees, community,

investors, customers, sales—normally are supplemented by
certain other specialized groups or publics. These other publics are unique to certain companies.

Other specialized publics—groups requiring personalized
appeals and programming—include such audiences as opinion leaders (3 percent of our population); ethnic groups;
labor organizations; travel agents; and youth groups, to
name only a few.

Can you always reach a particular public for your company or client? Absolutely—one way or another! There are
two fundamental factors to remember: First, you must define the public or publics your company wants to communicate with. Second, you carefully select the best techniques
and public relations tools at your command to "talk to" the
public you want to reach.

5 PR Goes to Press— Working with Newspapers

Your ability to work with the press will determine how effective a public relations person you are. It's absolutely basic to your business.

The press means all the print media, of course—newspapers, magazines, syndicates and wire services. Each has its specific character and requisites.

First, let's look at newspaper publicity. The ability to be a good reporter, to be able to service newspapers with valid, newsworthy material usually is a requirement for anyone who wants to be successful in public relations.

Why are newspapers so important to public relations activity? They're part of a whole, in terms of PR programming. The single most important reason that newspapers are important to you as a PR hopeful, however, is the demands they make upon you.

To work well with newspapers means you must be a good publicist. You must know the fundamentals of good reporting and be able to write the facts in clear, concise, journalistic style. You must know what kind of copy a newspaper will use and what is a throw-away to an editor. To be a good reporter requires considerable discipline: your story must be news or it must create news; it must be written sparingly, cover all the facts; timing must be on target. News about a new product must coincide with its availability locally; nothing is more irritating to an editor than to run a story about a new product and have readers complain that they can't find it in stores. Granted the editor should have checked local stores, but *your* job is to save him this step and be sure that when he checks, the item is on the shelves, ready to go.

A young PR trainee, working for the first time at a public relations agency, Edward Gottlieb Associates (rated by *Editor & Publisher* as one of this country's top ten), went into PR from an editorial job on a consumer magazine. One of her early assignments was to write a fashion release for a client. The copy she turned in was mediocre. In her anxiety to do the job quickly, she failed to evaluate the copy properly: Did it tell the entire story? Were all aspects of the story covered—what was new, what fabric was used, why these particular fashions differed from any other line? The account executive pointed out how loosely organized the material was and that important facts were missing.

The PR junior listened intently, then brightened as she replied to her boss, "Oh. You mean there should be more *sell* in the copy."

Call it sell, then! But always include the basic five W's— Who, What, When, Where and Why. This means you might have to dig a bit and find out all the facts. *Why* did your company, an insecticide firm, come up with a dandelion-dehydrant for the first time, when they've been in business for twenty-five years?

A good publicist should be even more diligent than a good reporter. He must anticipate the questions a reporter will want answered as well as those of the ultimate readers.

How can you spot good newspaper writing? Look at your local paper; study it carefully. The big news stories on page 1 often have an international dateline and wire-service credit, such as Paris, March 7 (UPI). Read the first three paragraphs and notice how much information is packed into a small space.

Then turn to a local news story. Read the first three paragraphs and compare the essential information given with that of the big news story. If your local paper is staffed by good, intelligent reporters, the local copy will cover the important facts just as thoroughly as the major news story serviced from a special news source in a big city. Every story in your paper is about an event, a situation, a person, or a product. Technically, every article is *some* kind of publicity! Consider, for instance, the lead story in *The New York Times* on June 5, 1966:

GEMINI POSTPONES
A 'WALK' IN SPACE:
DOCKING CANCELLED

The Cape Kennedy-datelined story reported a last-minute change in plans for astronauts Cernan and Stafford, and the reasons why. Who is the "publicity" for? The U. S. Government Space program, in its race to the moon.

Flip several pages of the same paper, and pause on page 68: *Seat Belt Improvement Urged*. This small news story recommended that all cars be equipped with a standardized seat belt. Who is the publicity for? Both the National Safety Council and the Society of Automotive Engineers were mentioned in the release.

You'll find similar stories in your own local paper; the datelines change, the information sources or credits will vary—but whether it's a political personality, a party program, a new kind of reducing machine or someone getting married, each and every article in your paper is some kind of publicity.

Next question: what value is newspaper publicity today?

Answer: "Incalculable!" The vital importance of newspapers in our daily lives bears some consideration because newspapers are as basic as breakfast. Whether you have coffee only or a full-course meal, it's a regular happening!

Just about every literate American reads one newspaper every day. The American Newspapers Publishers Association estimates that on an average week day approximately 89,567,000 adults read a newspaper and about 73,833,000 adults read a Sunday paper. Also, according to the ANPA, circulation of papers is at an all-time high: more than 60,-537,563 daily subscribers.

Editor & Publisher notes there are about 1,751 dailies, a black-and-white habit with millions of Americans. Your local daily paper *is* a habit—even the way you read it becomes a highly personalized ritual. You may start on page one and go through your paper carefully, or you may note big news on page one, then skip to your favorite column or feature. But you *do* read the paper, and you usually do so daily. Thus the news you note is absorbed or discarded, but an impression is created, whether you consciously know it or not. Also, each of us reacts to a subject with varying degrees of interest or concern. A golfer, for example, will read columns about the golf tournament, but he'll pay little or no attention to a long feature on a local flower show. His wife, on the other hand, probably will ignore the golf story, but she'll clip the article that tells her how to arrange roses as demonstrated at the local flower show.

Both the golf tournament and the flower show undoubtedly had specific people handling the press relations. The PR pro—and put yourself in his place—would know the news angles for the newspaper, and he'd know which department should get the story. Obviously, golf news is sports page material. And flower show news? Women's page editors would be most interested, because women would be primarily drawn to the event. A pro would service the city desk, as well, because certain events at a local flower show might be of general news interest.

Every newspaper has certain departments or sections— and every company or client has news or products of interest to a particular department. Get to know the different areas of a paper, then direct your copy to that specific section. *Editor & Publisher* produces a yearbook that's a vital tool to most publicity people, because the major dailies of every city in the United States are listed, with the proper editor for a specific department. You might not always use the editor's name but you certainly should have the correct editorial department for your story. Most dailies have these departments or sections, and each has its own requirements for copy. You need not be reminded that an automotive editor wants different material from a travel editor. Even though your client may be the state of Maine—and nearly everyone who goes there drives there—a completely different news angle is needed for each editor.

Check your own paper and see how many of these departments you find "covered" by your paper:

Amusements
Automotive
Books
Business-Financial
Education
Food
Garden
Home Furnishings
Radio-TV
Real Estate
Religion
Science
Society
Sports
Travel

Depending on the size of your city, your daily paper will have departments and news on each of these categories— and perhaps others, as well. Getting a daily paper together is a tremendous job, and as an able publicist you can help the reporters and editors do their jobs.

Just how much do newspapers use public relations and publicity releases? Again, it depends on the paper—some use more than others. Studies have been made to determine the source of news in daily newspapers, and the conclusion is that every major daily in the country does use publicity material—ranging from one-third of the news presented to as high as 80 percent of the entire editorial content.

Don't think it will be too easy, however, to gain a good reputation with editors. You earn it, by proving that the stories you provide are accurate and interesting. Earning a good reputation with the working press may take a while. Editors are prone to be highly critical of publicity people, and often with good reason. Aileen Ryan, former Women's Editor of one of the largest dailies in America, The Milwaukee *Journal,* is explicit in her views about PR and publicists:

"Most PR people don't know anything about a newspaper. They've never worked on one—they really don't know what's going on—how a paper operates. Maybe that's why most PR people think they have to entertain the press. Their ultimate idea of working [with the press] is a "junket"—a free trip.

"I believe everyone in PR should work for a newspaper at least one year," Miss Ryan asserts. "There are only a handful of people in New York, Chicago or Milwaukee who know what they're doing, or what *we're* doing.

"Newspapers want news. We don't get truthful information about products from most PR people. We need accurate, updated information, and it shouldn't go to six different people on the same newspaper."

Miss Ryan, a commanding woman with soft wavy gray hair and sparkling blue eyes, directs all activities on the distaff side of her paper; she and her staff are besieged by PR people "wanting something for nothing," and with hundreds of "news" releases that are discarded each day.

"We simply don't have time to look at everything that comes over our desk. Publicity people waste time and money sending out too much material. They'd do much better to send one good, valid news story."

How does most copy come through to papers? Sloppy, is the consensus.

"The caliber of writing is poor," Miss Ryan says. "Most PR releases have no facts. And a common failing of publicity releases is over-writing."

The carelessness of many public relations people in their dealings with editors of the nation's press is obvious after talking with a few editors of different papers. Multiple mailings to the same paper—identical releases to several people on one staff—are a common fault.

The Women's page Editor of the Oklahoma City *Daily Oklahoman*, Joan Gilmore, reports that her paper has requested that only *one* mailing on a specific subject be sent to her paper, and the paper has written various PR agencies and firms asking that publicity be handled this way.

"Often we've written the same companies two or three times, suggesting they change their mailing lists. We even give them the name of the editor who should get the material. Know what happens? The *new* name is added—and six of the people on the original mailing list still get the release, too.

"Very few companies even bother to acknowledge our requests. One did, though—the federal government. After we had sent three notes asking that releases be sent to a particular editor, we got an answer. The department in Washington wrote that 'We always send you twenty releases. Which *one* do you want stopped?' "

Most of the editors questioned were unanimous in their

view that public relations people waste money: duplication of mailings, too many photos, poor quality, second-rate copy and sloppy mailing lists. Lloyd Stewart of the Ft. Worth *Star Telegram* reported that the department's mail indicated some mailing lists haven't been updated in 15 years.

The attitudes of women's page editors are important for two fundamental reasons: these editors' comments reflect *all* departmental editors' views, from the city desk to sports editors. Secondly, nearly every product made is directed to or bought by women. Women are responsible for over 90 percent of all the purchases made in this country. Accordingly, most publicists automatically think they should send a release to the women's page editors, without too much thought about the newspapers, the geography, the availability of the product—or, apparently, the caliber of the release. Maybe the client or company makes only oil filters. Use some fancy words, a publicist decides—cute copy—and the wife will send her husband out to buy the oil filter. Sound thinking?

Perhaps your client sells sweaters—obviously a woman's page item. So what do you do? You gather publicity photos (more about printable photos later), collect frothy thoughts on sweaters and pack off hundreds of envelopes to women's page editors. Did you tell each where her readers could buy the garment? Probably not. Did you give any advice about care of the sweater—how to wash it, how to mix-and-match it with various kinds of clothing? Or did you prepare just another throw-away release containing paragraphs strung together with no particular order, no facts, no service, no reason to interest an editor or a reader?

If you're going to be a pro in PR, read your newspaper carefully, and then sharpen your editing pencils!

The basics for working effectively with any newspaper—whether it's a metropolitan paper or a small daily in the heart of the Midwest—are the same. You must know what you're talking about, have sound knowledge of your subject, and you must present it in professional form.

Naturally, individual papers vary. The Miami *Herald* will have different editorial requirements from the Appleton (Wisconsin) *Post Crescent*. The *Herald* will carry more sophisticated, general interest material, for example. It's up to you to learn the differences if you want to be a better than run-of-the-mill publicity person.

Here's a checklist to follow when you're preparing release material for a consumer newspaper. Follow these rules, and you'll be better prepared for your career in public relations:

—Know the media you're trying to reach. Study the specific publications; read papers from different areas of the country. Learn what type of news is printed and what isn't. Use this knowledge as a guideline for preparing your own material.

—Present your news in professional form. Write clear, concise newspaper copy. Give all the facts and only the facts. This doesn't mean dull, heavy-going copy; use your ingenuity, and present the facts and story in a fresh, interesting manner. (Your own paper isn't dull, it's sharp, good reading. How about your own release? Would *you* read it— not to say print it—if you were an editor?)

—Learn the different departments of a paper. Direct your copy to the right department. Remember that one copy of a release per paper is enough.

—Always be reliable. The press learns whom they can depend on, and whom they can't. Build your reputation with the press as a person who can be trusted for accuracy, reliability, complete fairness and dependability.

—*Timing is vital.* News is *now*—of the moment. Editors want news, even for feature material. If you're talking about new products, they should be available locally. If you're offering suggestions, to a homeowner or a sports car driver, they should be timely and in proper season. Remember your role as a reporter. Editors want to know what's new, what's ahead, when and why. Your job—report the facts, fully and professionally.

—Now go rework that copy. You know it can be better and more interesting, not just another publicity "throw-away!"

6 Read All About It—
All Kinds of Papers

"All right, Frank. You know the story. Suppose you draft a program covering next year's publicity plans. Stick to the print media, okay? How soon can you pull this together so we can review it?"

You heard your boss! Tell him you'll have a tentative program outlined for him in two days—and that means getting your regular work out, as well.

You've been working for several months in the public relations department of The Arkay Precision Instrument Company; your particular group handles PR for consumer products, primarily those of the company division that makes hi-fi components. Now your company has come up with a remarkable new product for hi-fi equipment, one that will make present sets obsolete and will be available to the public within six months. Outlining a newspaper publicity program should be a challenge to you. Are you ready?

Maybe not, according to Harold Herman, executive vice-president of Racal Communications.

"The real trouble is that the PR man doesn't have the

know-how to service a highly technical field such as electronics."

To succeed in tomorrow's world of public relations, you're going to need a lot of know-how, a sound working knowledge of the area you've chosen for your special field. If it's electronics, knowledge of that industry is fundamental, and you'll have to work to keep up with the continuing developments in this dynamic field.

Let's assume you do have the necessary technical knowledge and skills essential to understand the field, and you're in public relations. That means you must be able to translate the complex, technical facts into everyday language without losing anything in translation.

You know about publics; you know how to define them and the importance of reaching and informing the *right* public for your company. Now your job is to prepare a program designed to reach that specific public, within the framework of print media—all the newspapers, consumer and trade, that would be interested in news and information about your company's products. (Magazines are a different category and not yet your concern; that's your *next* job!)

To do a saturation publicity job for your company covering every possible newspaper outlet with properly directed material, you begin by reviewing the publics you want to reach, then consider the outlets available to you to reach these particular publics.

No matter what product or idea your company wants to sell or tell, there's a publication catering to the specific interests, whether you're dealing with hi-fi components, enriched corn meal, outboard motors, foreign sportscars, or perhaps a political candidate. Your first job is to know all you can about your company and product, then to feed information into the many channels available to you for publication of news about your company's product.

National syndicates. One of the most effective methods of

reaching a specific audience or public is through one of the editorial syndicate services. One syndicate story reaches a great number of newspapers; your one story, well done, goes to thousands of readers.

There's a syndicate for almost every idea that can be put down on paper. Syndicates, the dictionary reports, are "organizations that sell special articles to different newspapers for simultaneous publication."

Any PR person will confirm half of this definition—but "simultaneous publication" is far from accurate. A syndicate may suggest that an editor or paper use a particular feature at a given time, but the choice of publication date is entirely the editor's prerogative. Often clippings have been returned as long as a year after the release date suggested by the syndicate.

This means that when you submit material to a syndicate, it must remain exclusive to that syndicate for all time. There's no re-using it later.

Syndicates are an important media for PR people because they're an important news source to their subscribing newspapers. They provide their papers with special, exclusive material the editors can't or don't get locally, covering nearly every conceivable subject.

Editor & Publisher puts out an annual Directory of Syndicated Newspaper Features, which includes the names and contact points for more than 280 different syndicates. This directory also lists forty-one different classifications of features, with lierally hundreds of individual columns within the categories.

If you're a clever, ingenious reporter, there's a syndicate column category that could be a news outlet for your company's information, whether it's business-financial, farm news, science or women's page material.

The effective PR person learns how the different syndicates work, what kind of material each uses, and what timing is important. (Normally, syndicates and daily newspapers require different timing.) It's a big job, but like using library stacks, it's simple and extremely productive once you learn how!

Do most public relations people know how to work with syndicates? "Too many are concerned with their own narrow point of view," executive editor Robert Roy Metz of Newspaper Enterprise of America asserts. NEA is one of this country's largest editorial feature syndicates, servicing hundreds of papers daily throughout the country.

"For instance, General Motors should be interested in broadening the motor market—not just pushing a particular make of car. We're interested in a PR person who has a trend story, a modern living point of view—not just his narrow product story."

Mr. Metz says that he has been reading "handouts"—editorial jargon for PR releases—for more than fifteen years.

"The quality of writing has improved, generally, but most newspaper people won't use a handout as such. They'll rework the lead, sometimes the body copy. So we look for writing that's professional. NEA looks for clarity, integrity and thoroughness.

"There's a growing need for good PR people. We're living in an increasingly complex world. The population is better and better educated. PR people can serve a real editorial need by being sound reporters, analysts, accurate interpreters of what's going on.

"If you're trying to sell me a story, here's what I'd want to know." Mr. Metz cited these elements, to be outlined in memo form:

—tell story line
—give basic background
—include material published on the subject
—provide leads on people editor can interview or check with on subject

Mr. Metz also had some advice for young people interested in public relations:

"Personality has a lot to do with it! We'd rather work with a friendly, relaxed person, someone who won't push you. And be proud of your field. Too often we get folks who begin by telling us they used to be newspaper men.

"Believe in what you're doing. If you don't, you belong in another business."

The way you work with any syndicate is comparable to how you work with newspapers directly—in terms of technical competence. Your material must be newsworthy, accurate, properly and professionally presented. So whether your story is slanted for NEA's women's pages, the food pages of Associated Press, the "Financial Gossip" column of United Press International, or to make the "Hollywood Everywhere" column, syndicated by North American Newspaper Alliance, Inc., it must be clear, accurate and have a news angle.

Another member of the syndicate fraternity—and of importance to the PR person planning a total publicity program —is the supplement section put out by newspapers. In the strictest sense, these are not syndicates. Yet, in fact, a nationally distributed newspaper magazine goes to many sections of the country and contains a great diversity of material.

Magazine supplements. If you live in Akron, Milwaukee or Abilene (Texas), you know your Sunday paper includes the magazine "This Week." Other cities' papers offer "Parade," or perhaps "Family Weekly." Study the magazine delivered with your Sunday paper; get to know the kind of editorial material it uses. Send away for copies of the other nationally distributed newspaper magazines, and notice how they differ. In addition to those mentioned, there are "American Weekly," "Suburbia Today," and "Tone."

When you've studied each and know the editorial requirements of each—how they're alike and how they differ—then you're in a position to contact the right editor about your company, client or product. Be sure you know what you're talking about before you contact him, however. He'll know in a hurry if you really read his material—or if you're just shooting in the dark!

Here's one example of how PR programming worked with one of the departments at "This Week." There's a regular column or department called "Bonanza," telling readers what's new and offering booklets about it. One week the column might talk about a new wonder diet, a safety feature for cars, a camp site in Maine, or how to knit an Irish sweater. Readers are invited to write in for free booklets about the particular column item. The Bernat Yarn company offered instruction leaflets to knitters, telling them how to knit genuine fishermen's sweaters in Irish yarn. Nearly 10,000 requests were received for the instruction leaflets—and that's a lot of yarn.

Weekly newspapers. Another important medium for publicity planning is weeklies. There are 8,003 weekly newspapers in the United States published in towns under 50,000 population. Total readership of these weeklies is growing. In 1966, more than twenty-six million Americans read a weekly paper every week. This is hometown, U.S.A.—and a powerful potential outlet for news and stories.

There's a vital difference between most dailies and weeklies: news must have a local angle for the weeklies. In larger cities, news, events and products often merit editorial attention because of what they are—the general reader is interested. Weeklies are different: an event is news only when its local.

Circus coming to town? It's better news if the mayor welcomes the group! Even a new car has its local angle: who sells it, what about the local dealer? Maybe he'll offer a new car for charity use one day a week.

Discovering the local angle or news aspect for weeklies

often is difficult and time-consuming for the publicity man, but the results usually warrant the effort. People do read these papers carefully. They often have greater influence over readers than big-city papers.

One unusual and effective method of working with local papers, both dailies and weeklies, was a project planned by the account supervisor for Florists' Transworld Delivery, Joe Daley—also a senior vice-president at Edward Gottlieb Associates. Mr. Daley conceived a plan for FTD that would focus attention on sending flowers by wire for Mother's Day.

Arrangements were made for every governor's wife in the country to receive a huge bouquet from someone in Washington, D.C., to honor her on Mother's Day. Each governor's press secretary was contacted in advance and advised of the project, and a special photographer was assigned by Daley's PR firm to photograph the First Lady of each state.

Then the wire service of each state—such as AP or UPI—was provided with the timely news material. Since most of the papers in a state subscribe to a major wire service, papers throughout each state received their respective First Family's photograph showing their own First Lady being presented with a thoughtful bouquet on Mother's Day!

Each photo was captioned with the fact the flowers had been wired as a tribute from a political personage in Washington—enough of a "plug" for FTD, a nonprofit organization. This project resulted in good publicity for the organization, it reminded readers to send flowers, and it was a thoughtful gesture to fifty leading mothers on "their" day. PR at work—and well!

Mat services. Still another means of reaching that tremendous number of Americans who live in suburban and rural areas—more than fifty-four million, according to the census of 1964—is through mat releases.

Technically, a mat, or matrix, is a papier-mâché impression of type and any artwork from which a plate can be made for printing. Many small publications have equipment for making lead castings from a mat for their papers but are not equipped to make plates from original photos or layouts.

The reason for using mat releases is to get your story into smaller publications, both rural and suburban papers, that normally wouldn't use original material because of their limited reproducton facilities.

You can prepare your own mat material and send it directly to the thousands of publications that require their news and features in this form. Or you can work with one of the many mat distribution firms, that specialize in this business.

Although you pay for this commercial service, you're still competing for editorial space with the major agencies and big companies who also want to reach this particular newspaper-reading public. So your material must be good. The more you know about your business, the better you'll be able to judge the caliber of the mat material you send out. This assumes you've taken the time and effort to read a number of smaller weeklies and "little publications," of course. From now on, it should be axiomatic for anyone interested in the public relations business to spend time studying the various print media and learning the requirements of each. A little extra reading never hurt anyone!

Foreign language press. Today more than sixty-seven foreign language dailies are published, plus a number of weeklies. As the number of foreign-born people in our country increases, and as more Americans become bilingual, this special press area will become increasingly important in public relations work.

When you want to reach specific ethnic groups, their own newspapers may be the key. If you're fluent in a second language, this too will be a great asset to you professionally. If your company wants to interest Italian-Americans in leather products from Firenze, as part of a general public relations program, you'll be of greater service to the Italian newspaper editors when you talk their language, especially if you also write in a professional journalistic style. The interviews you arrange with officials from the company, with key civic officials, as well as the consular corps, will be highly beneficial to the effective public relations planning for your company.

If you know a second language now, pick up a paper published in that language; read it, study it, and decide whether it is a useful means of relaying news or a series of messages to a particular group.

The Foreign Language Press of America, 10 East 43rd Street, New York, N. Y., can supply you with a listing of major foreign dailies printed in this country.

"You Oughta be in Pictures." You *ought* to be, if you're serious about public relations. But too often PR people are painfully ignorant of this vital area.

Ruby Weil, one of the editors of Associated Press's Wide World Picture department, who has worked with pictures, photographers and publicity people for years, says flatly that "too many PR people don't know anything about pictures!

"For instance," she said, "they don't even know what an original negative is."

How about glossies, matte finishes, multiple prints and contrast? All these terms should be part of your vocabulary, your *working* vocabulary.

Mrs. Weil had more comments about PR people and their knowledge of pictures:

"Pictures must be in focus. And composition must be good. But focus—that's vital."

It's hard to believe anyone active in this business would submit a photograph for publication that's *not* in focus, but judging from this picture editor's vehemence, too many public relations people just don't know enough about this aspect of their business. Your future in PR will be brighter if you're in focus, photographically speaking!

One cardinal rule for your career in public relations is this: learn all you can about photography, the fundamental mechanics of what makes a good picture. Familiarize yourself with the basics—red becomes black and pastels wash out in black-and-white photos. Take a course in photography, work in a darkroom, read books about it; whatever time you invest now in learning all you can about photography and picture reproduction will pay off handsomely for you.

When you're on your PR job, ask the picture editor what he requires before you approach him with photos; the first time around, he'll be pleased to advise you what his newspaper or syndicate needs. The *second* time, forget it!

Photo captions are capsule news reports. All the information should be there—succinct, clear, brief. Your captions should run four typed lines, no longer. Put in all the facts, forget flowery adjectives, keep your copy to the point. In short, be professional.

Business and Trade Newspapers. Frank's proposed program for Arkay's new hi-fi component probably includes plans for coverage in the business and trade newspapers. If his company is publicly held—that is, if shares of stock are for sale to the general public—he'll be smart to prepare special stories for powerful business newspapers such as the *Wall Street Journal* and *Barron's*.

Today, business is news. Millions of Americans own shares in corporations, and with their own money invested in this way, they want to know all about American business in general. They are even more eager for news about firms into which they have put their money.

Dramatic proof of the public's interest in business is the fact that the *Wall Street Journal* is America's second most popular newspaper. Its circulation is topped only by New York's tabloid—the New York *Daily News*. Maybe this indicates that second to sensationalism, readers are interested in business!

In addition to the business and finance weeklies such as *Barron's* and the dailies such as the *Wall Street Journal, Journal of Commerce* and Los Angeles *Commercial News*, there are also daily papers serving particular industries. Examples are the Fairchild Publications, including: *Women's Wear Daily, Home Furnishings Daily, Footwear News*.

Frank also will want to get his story on the Dow Jones news wire, a teletype network concentrating on business news. Subscribers to the service include daily newspapers, stock brokers, individual corporations.

What type of story suits these special dailies? Frank's outline will indicate it. Generally, for the business newspapers, it must be a more detailed story than that for the daily papers. He will explain the scientific breakthrough in depth. But more than that, he will have to interview his own top management to get the facts on what this new product means for the company's financial future.

He'll find out how much it cost to develop this new product, when mass production will start, what the marketing plans are, what the potential sales may be, how much this may contribute to earnings next year, what this means per share of stock. Men and women who have invested in Arkay want to know what they can expect in dividends and increased value of their stock. Other investors want the facts before they buy shares or sell them.

The financial PR man has to be particularly conscientious and thorough in getting the facts clearly and accurately. Not only does he have to protect his company's reputation for truthful reporting, but also there are federal laws regulating this type of reporting. The Securities & Exchange Commission has laid down guidelines to prevent either inadequate disclosure or reporting that exaggerates in order to attract investors' dollars.

Working with the editors. Just how do you "work with the press"—whether it's consumer press or business publications? You'll work directly, very often on a personal basis, particularly if you live in one of the metropolitan communication centers, such as New York, Chicago, or San Francisco. All the major news services have offices in the large cities and these funnel information to the nation.

You'll learn how the individual editors prefer to work with PR people—a query by letter or a fast call on the phone. You'll become oriented to the requirements of the individual editors, the publications and the syndicates. You'll learn their graphic or photographic preferences, and the deadlines. Some syndicates work a month ahead; some longer. The business periodicals work close to deadline, particularly on a hot news item; you must learn all these basics.

You'll also work with out-of-town editors on an individual paper basis, via meetings, letters and phone; also, you'll "work" via regular, consistent mailings to editors throughout the country. Mailings—distribution of photos and releases to a specific department of a paper—should be as professional as possible: clear, fact-filled news releases with sharp, reproducible pictures. These are mechanical details, but an understanding of them separates the men from the boys.

There is a feeling that there is far too much use and abuse of press contacts in PR activity. You will get to know editors, many of them well, but to prevail upon friendship as a means for "peddling a story" is a sorry commentary on two legitimate professions—yours and theirs.

The qualities an editor looks for in a public relations person, consciously or unconsciously, are summed up in these basic five:

—integrity
—accuracy
—dependability
—thoroughness
—resourcefulness

Develop all five qualities; start right now; and you'll grow into a fine human being, first of all; you'll also earn the kind of reputation that is being enjoyed by the top men and women in public relations today.

7 PR in Print—
Working with Magazines

The girl with the round, owl-like dark glasses hurried through the noisy crowd milling in the sun on New York's Seventh Avenue. She looked like an illustration from a fashion magazine, the very epitome of today's high fashion. She clearly was a "Magazine Girl" from a fashion magazine.

She was en route to a fashion collection in the garment district, and following the chic showing she would meet Andrew for lunch at a new French bistro. Andrew worked for another magazine—one of the big weekly news publications. He had blond hair turning darker, was medium height, stocky; Andrew was a good writer and was being groomed for an associate editor post. Both Andrew and the Magazine Girl work in that glamorous world of NOW, the cadence of their calendars marked by the publication of their respective periodicals. Each conforms to the pattern of his own publication—she almost unreal and glossy, he carefully undistinguished, nearly nondescript, but with a definite erudite look which he cultivates.

Their worlds are created by the people who populate the

mastheads of magazines. This world can be yours, too, in a less involved way, when you're in public relations.

You can enjoy the excitement, the urgency and uniqueness of the magazine world without literally being a part of it. This is another privilege of PR people. You see, your special knowledge, your access to facts and information, and your ability to get to the decision-making people within your organization or client company often is a valuable aid to enterprising editors. And as publications become more specialized, your liaison role and fact-finding abilities will become even more important to the magazines.

Working with magazines is often an enjoyable, pleasant and rewarding task. It also can be irritating. From the conception, acceptance and development of an idea until it finally appears in print can be a long and tiresome tour of duty. It can require endless research, infinite patience, sometimes careful cajoling—even total "hands off" an idea that originally was yours. Tact is requisite!

But when you finally read your own suggestion or story line in print, it's usually personally satisfying. This is an incidental emotional reaction, however, that's merely part of the game.

The publication of any article, though it may have been months in gestation, is just the beginning for the PR man. For a magazine article, feature or column to be of value to a company or client, it must meet three basic requirements. All reflect your efforts, planning and skill:

THE AUDIENCE MUST BE ON TARGET. The story or article must appear in a publication directed to and read by the public your company or client wants to reach. (A good, meaty article on computers, quoting your company's comptroller, appearing in the *Farm Journal* might just get you your walking papers. The same article in *The Nation's Business* could earn a raise and move you up to cloud nine!)

TIMING MUST BE RIGHT. The editorial commentary must be coordinated with the company's marketing planning and programming. If the story involves a product, for instance, that product must be available to readers when they read about it—whether it's a new car model, hair dryer or hunting boots. The season must be as right as the availability; who needs those new hunting boots in June? A feature that jumps the gun on distribution is of little value to your company.

THE ARTICLE MUST BE MERCHANDISABLE. To read about your new product, your company or an idea voiced by an officer of your firm is just the beginning. It must have some repeat value: can it be reprinted for your company's salesmen? Is it worth sending to potential customers? Can your management quote it to their stockholders? As public relations activity moves more strongly into the total marketing picture, the "merchandising" aspects of magazine and publication copy will become even more important.

To illustrate a semi-loss of good public relations effort because of poor editorial presentation, consider a story that ran in a major magazine. An equipment manufacturer hoped to promote, through a good magazine article, its new color line. Arrangements were made to transform a dilapidated old kitchen area into a modern miracle, a kitchen of tomorrow, using the firms equipment. A sparkling new stove, refrigerator, dishwasher; and a smart laundry, was tucked behind louvered doors in one section of the room.

Then the editors worked long hours to get just the right light and mood for their readers. The kitchen was photographed in color as well as black-and-white.

When the story was laid out, the key photograph in color depicted the one section of the kitchen devoid of any equipment! The chosen color photograph admittedly was handsome editorially, but the value of the story to the company was considerably lessened. Yet the promotion department of the magazine couldn't understand why it didn't order thousands of reprints; after all, the equipment was shown in several black-and-white shots. The PR department had to remind them, gently, that the color of the equipment was the real news!

This example of PR working with a national magazine met two of the vital three basics very well: the audience was on target and timing was right.

The third PR requirement—merchandisability—was not met. Certainly the feature was of value to the manufacturer, but not to the degree possible if the magazine had selected a different picture to feature, one with a suggestion of the equipment in it. (The reason for the story, initially!)

Could the PR department have handled the situation differently? PR provided the idea—renovation of an old house into a practical, modern convenience story; PR arranged for the architect as well as the affluent owner who paid all the costs. The agency also made whatever arrangements the editors desired to facilitate the shooting schedule. That's all it should do. If public relations, or any group, attempts to dictate any press decisions, that spells trouble. To work with any media—magazines, publications, newspapers, even radio or TV—means to provide accurate, timely, needed information. Suggesting when the material might best be used is the extent of any such recommendations. No one on the editorial side likes any kind of pressure, nor should they have it.

Your job in PR will be much smoother if you tell yourself each morning: "Never *tell* an editor how to work. Never."

Should you forget, try it. See how far you get—toward the door!

How do you work with a magazine? Careful planning is the key, planning directed to a specific publication. General ideas are of little or no value in planning any magazine publicity. You must *know* the publication you're aiming for—

read it, study back issues, really know the kind of material it uses. And then submit only article ideas which suit the style of the magazine.

There are about four hundred monthly magazines in this country, covering every conceivable subject. It's an age of specialization, remember. There has been a rise in special interest magazines and a fall in general interest "books." Whether it's directed toward antiques, home interests, hobbies or health, today there's a weekly or monthly magazine devoted exclusively to the subject. You name it, and there's a magazine about it!

In addition to the hundreds of monthly magazines, there are literally thousands of company and trade publications catering to special-interest areas. Part of your job in public relations will be to discover the magazines—both major and minor publications—that are concerned with your company's or client's interests. Do they reach the publics your company wants to reach? Do they inform and influence? If so, then your job is to see how journalistically creative you can be. What will interest the editor?

There are plenty of tools to help you initially: *Bacon's Publicity Checker*, for example, lists all major consumer and trade magazines by category; *The Gebbie Press House Magazine Directory* lists the more than four thousand house organs. The *New York Publicity Outlets* booklet covers all the major magazines published in New York City and lists various departments and names of editors.

Consumer magazine classifications. To give you a specific idea of the special interest areas of specific magazines, here's a partial listing of the categories with several different magazines published in each:

—*Business and finance. Fortune, Business Week, Forbes, Journal of Commerce* are only a few of the many business-directed publications. This is a specialized area and requires extensive, thorough knowledge on your part. Chapter nine discusses the field of financial public relations—what you need to know to work effectively with the editors of business and financial publications.

—*Entertainment.* An entire group of magazines is devoted to various aspects of the "lively" arts—music, show business, personalities, dance, radio, television and theatre. Check the list in *Bacon's;* if your company or client can contribute in any way to the editorial form of a given magazine, you undoubtedly can work with the editor.

The role of press agents and publicists associated with entertainment and personalities is a changing one today. It's becoming more respectable. This is one area where fast talkers have capitalized on the "Publicist" or PR label—without he ability, skill, or integrity to back it up. Fortunately, this kind of character is disappearing as the ranks of publicity and public relations grow with bright, ambitious and conscientious young people.

One story still circulates about the novice in publicity who was star-struck by the personality clients of an American-born "Italian Count" who directed a small PR agency in New York City for a period of time. The boy worked for three weeks with the agency, learning the ropes and various press contacts the agency worked with. After three weeks, he spoke with the Count about his paycheck—when could he expect it? "Why, you're working with us for the *experience!*" he was told. The boy left, to gain experience in a more creditable agency and also get paid for his efforts.

—*General interest.* This category is disappearing, as mentioned, to become channeled into specific types. However, there's still *The Saturday Evening Post, National Geographic,* and *Pageant,* to name a few. Their editorial coverage is general and reaches a large audience. By the time you're ready to approach these magazines, however, their editorial policies may have changed. They too may become "special" rather than general interest.

—*Home interest.* Publications of this category often stress service-oriented copy. Does your company have a valid "how to" angle that would be of interest to home and apartment dwellers? If so, you might have a magazine story possibility to explore.

The area of interest could be anything from decorating to French champagne, depending on the editorial range of the publication and your own resourcefulness in editorial suggestions. Keep your ideas plausible; a home-interest publication would not be likely to consider a strictly religious-focused feature.

—*Men's magazines.* This category has increased with the advent of *Playboy* into the field. Men's products, interests, fashions and people themselves are all editorial possibilities. *Esquire,* one of the giants, actually *requests* material from PR people! For example, each June the Gift/Shopping editor, Virginia Reilly, writes to companies and agencies asking if there's "something new you'd like to submit for consideration . . ." and closing with "looking forward to hearing from you and working with you to make this Christmas issue *Esquire's* best, ever." Here's a top magazine using PR techniques—requesting information, all the facts, and making it a pleasure to work with the editor!

—*Motion picture, romance magazines.* A large number of publications cater to the tremendous number of readers who want to read about Bobby Darin, the Denims, the latest Hollywood news—even Cary Grant! A surprisingly large number of magazines are also published for a reading public who get the romance in their life from printed pages. "My Son—Born Without a Father" sounds like lurid reading, but often the titles of stories in romance books are racier than their content. Thousands buy and read these magazines. If your company produces a mass-market product—say food, tires, proprietary drugs—then these magazines might be one means to inform a large public.

—*News and picture magazines. Time, Newsweek, Life, Look, U. S. News and World Report* are all available to expert PR people who offer valid, timely news tips, marketing ideas, information on key personalities in the news or business headlines. When publications of this caliber are interested in following a lead to a story, they usually assign researchers to dig out facts; you may work with them— helping them see the "right" people, arranging interviews, making the researcher's efforts generally as easy as possible. You also might work with the reporter assigned, easing his way whenever possible. Your company's files might have useful photographs—you get them out for the reporter. Your knowledge of the company, the competition, and your access to people and facts are important in working effectively with news magazines. Usually they want everything immediately; you get it. Then the story might be bumped because a more vital news event happens in the same field of interest. Say your feature is on marketing washing machines. The week it's scheduled the head of a beauty product empire—an expert in marketing—dies. Your story is replaced with an obituary. The breaks of the game. It might or might not make it later, only *Time* will tell!

—*Outdoor living, sports.* These specialized fields are served by a number of publications. *Sport Illustrated* moved into this area with an editorial plan to appeal to the expanding popular interest in all kinds of sports. Today, more than eight million readers are devoted to this weekly, covering a range of subjects with a sporting aspect. Other publications such as *Yachting, Field & Stream, Sports Afield* serve special groups. Check *Bacon's* for the list of all publications in this category; does your company or client offer any products that might interest this big audience group? It's a big market potential for the resourceful PR person!

—*Parents and babies.* This category offers an audience well worth consideration if your company is involved in any way with products or services for this public. More than half the population of this country is under twenty-five—that means more young parents than ever (the average bride today is just under twenty) and consequently more babies! A number of publications are devoted to parents, babies, the cares and problems of each. If your company or client can relate to this huge slice of America, you can work with these magazines.

—Political and cultural. Many of the magazines in this group, primarily the second category, are non-illustrated publications read by the intelligentsia. Their readers are influential, those who lead the thinking of others. The cultural or intellectual magazines—*Atlantic, Commonweal, Harper's, The Reporter,* to name a few—are designed to stimulate thought, not sales. Does your company or client offer anything of an intellectually provocative nature? Perhaps an officer of the company is a renowned conservative. There's a market for his story, if it's within the framework of good public relations for the firm to have it reported.

—Religious. Nearly every denomination has a publication of its own, often with editorial opportunities for features not contrary to the predominate theme or principle. Check *Bacon's,* then the actual publications. The son of your company's board chairman, just returned from a stint with the Peace Corps, might also be active in his church group. *Presbyterian Life* might be interested in his views.

—Travel. Holiday, anyone? This is the most outstanding travel magazine in the consumer category, covering material well beyond travel, per se. (French Cognac's PR agency arranged for a writer to tour the vineyards of France, with a special Cognac story the result.) Today's travel magazines include broad editorial coverage—tips on how to travel, what to wear, etc., which offer wide publicity possibilities for ingenious PR workers.

—Women's magazines. Specialization is underscored in

the women's magazine area: today special publications are geared to upper-income fashionables (*Vogue* and *Harper's Bazaar*), to the working girl (*Glamour*), the college girl (*Mademoiselle*), the teenager (*Seventeen* and *Ingenue*), the single woman (*Cosmopolitan*), homemakers (*McCall's, Ladies' Home Journal, Redbook*)—to illustrate a few of the specific divisions within the general category of women's magazines. The content of these varied publications devoted to women confirms the scope of their interests: how to invest, where to send your children to college, how to raise children in a divorced home, space age advancements, the latest products of every kind. Nearly every thought and product has a woman's interest angle.

—*Youth publications.* Another long list of magazines specializing in juvenile interests is available for the checking. These magazines are read by the adults of tomorrow, and enterprising PR people appreciate the potential of this rich youth market. If your company or clients can relate in any logical way to the young market, there's considerable opportunity to work with the many magazines in this category.

These listings are just to give you an idea of the many categories of consumer publications there are today—and the list of specialties are growing.

Trade publications. The approach to trade publications hardly differs from consumers' magazines. Integrity, resourcefulness and professionalism are equally important in working with "the trades."

The primary difference between consumer and trade publications is that your knowledge must be even deeper and more technical for the professional and technical publications. The appeal of these magazines is more limited because they go to a strictly defined group of readers. You must spend time reading the trade publications that are relevant to your company's interests. If your firm is a drug company, you should read all the drug publications and many of the science magazines, particularly those covering scientific developments in the pharmaceutical field.

Suppose your company makes processed milk and you want to interest the readers of many different trade and professional publications in your product. How? Check categories relevant to food and food preparation in *Bacon's;* then request copies of the publications you think might be interested in information about your product. (Gratis copies usually are available when you write for them.)

Study the various publications. They'll probably range from supermarket booklets to those directed to restaurant and institution management. Some will be right for your product, some will not. But at least you'll *know.* When you've decided whether or not a publication is a possibility, decide if you can offer a sound angle for a story—perhaps an interview with your company nutritionist, a series of recipes in institution proportions, or perhaps an interview with your company comptroller, who's an expert in computers within his industry.

The point is, know your editorial target, whether it's a consumer or trade publication. Then tailor your material to that target. You'll be apt to hit a bull's-eye more often than not.

8 PR on Camera—
Wonderful World of TV

It's 6:20 A.M. The big second hand of the studio clock
swings its steady circle, marking another minute closer to
the moment many Americans recognize: 7 A.M., when the
"Today" show goes on the air again.

The hour before the nation's favorite wake-up show goes
on the air is frantic up on the sixth floor of the NBC building
at Rockefeller Plaza in New York City. The "regulars"—
Hugh Downs, Frank Blair and Barbara Walters—all must go
to make-up.

A skilled make-up artist gives both men and women a deft
touch of foundation base, powder; facial planes are softened
or accentuated. The show is in color, which means make-up
requirements are even more demanding.

One of the men returns to the make-up room wearing a
fresh light blue shirt. He has changed the white one he had
worn into the studio in favor of the blue, since the blue tele-
vises better in color and black and white.

On stage, across the corridor, set crews are moving props
into readiness so they can be placed in camera range at a
moment's notice during the show. Lights are tested—some

moved closer to the panel table, others wheeled across stage to blaze on the guest musicians at the given moment. There's an electric air of excitement, expectancy and urgency.

Hugh Downs adjusts his tie now and again, checks his watch—four more minutes—then strolls easily over to talk with the announcer, who is smoothing his dark hair with both hands. Both men—who seem as comfortable on camera as you are in your own living room—are obviously slightly nervous. Each morning, five days a week, they bring news, information and entertainment into millions of American homes. To them, their job is just that—a job! Yet despite their on-camera ease and knowledge of the medium, even skilled performers like "Today" show stars experience moments of anxiety before that second hand sweeps to the magic moment: 7 A.M. "Another opening, another show!"

Barbara Walters is ready now, short hair shining, make-up perfect, her dress properly casual and smart for that hour of the day. She too knows the moment is approaching: today she's going to interview three foreign floral designers, and she walks back and forth before the flower-laden display table, unaware of her own pacing!

Backstage, behind the lights and huge TV cameras, are "Today's" guests: the three floral designers and their PR girl; sixteen Boy Scouts—honor scouts from all parts of the country—and their leaders; a professorial type in a dark suit and a beard who turns out to be an actor playing George Bernard Shaw!

Lights flash, the people move into place, the stage quiets with an explosive silence, the floor director studies his watch, theme music sounds, a red light glows, the cameras roll as the director points emphatically at Hugh Downs, and another "Today" show begins!

Countless times a day, in every city of the nation, a similar scene is enacted as local TV shows get underway. The excitement, last-minute scurrying, frowns of script writers and directors are everyday fare in the frantic world of television.

Nearly every large city in the country has a television station—there are more than 500—and most have some original programming. Whether it's a major network show getting under way in New York, a newscaster in Bangor waiting for the red hand to sweep past the 12 on his studio clock, or a hostess of a homemaker's show in New Orleans waiting for the red light to appear on the No. 1 camera, it's show time, U.S.A., every hour of the day, in every city.

Public relations people share the drama and excitement of this fascinating world, too. Specialized knowledge is essential, of course, because you have to know some of the basics about the television business. But if you're fascinated by this stimulating world, there's opportunity for you in public relations. Depending on your own skills, abilities and experience, your work with television people can cover a considerable range—actual on-camera appearances, working with writers to give them background facts and information, scheduling guests on interview programs, preparing scripts, working with newsreel and film editors, or joining the PR department of a station or network.

The growth of the industry itself is noteworthy; within the past two decades, TV has spiraled to impressive heights. In 1960 there were more than forty-six million TV sets in homes alone; approximately 128 million people watched television every day, and for a startling number of hours. The average viewer looks at television six hours and eight minutes every day, according to the A. C. Nielson Company.

Prime-time television shows, with a good audience, capture more viewers than any other method of mass communication. One single top-rated TV show reaches a bigger audience than a famous movie does throughout all its reruns! (Excluding TV.)

Since all prime-time shows are sponsored, can public relations activity partake or contribute to such shows? Yes, indeed, through creative thinking, suggestions and knowledge of the medium. For example, one of the top-rated comedy shows during 1966 was the "Ozzie and Harriet Show."

During one of the programs, the theme centered on Harriet receiving a beautiful rose from an unknown admirer each day for a week. The situation developed from there. Ozzie stalked angrily into the local florist (complete with Flowers-By-Wire decal on the window) to demand the name of his wife's secret admirer.

Ozzie lost his courage in the shop, and the comedy continued in high gear for a full half-hour. The amusing show, with positive reviews from throughout the country, centered on sending flowers, the pleasure of receiving flowers—even Ozzie's chagrin over not knowing who sent them proved a pleasant situation comedy sequence.

The role of public relations? The agency handling flowers-by-wire had a live-wire account man in California who worked closely with the show's writers. The routine itself was suggested, although the show prepared its own material, of course; a bona-fide flower shop set was erected on the studio floor; and fresh flowers were provided—all the mock-shop could use!

The credit or return to the flowers-by-wire organization? A brief shot of the flower shop showing the association's golden mercury emblem in the window: a legitimate credit, which reached millions.

An additional public relations activity was pegged to this show. All the 11,000 FTD florist members were alerted, prior to show time, that this particular show would interest them. After the program, the floral trades magazines featured photographs and a story about the show. Thus the show itself, and its advertisers, had viewers they might not normally have claimed. And both the program and network received additional plugs from an unusual source—the floral trades publications and newsletter.

Another brief example of this same PR man's efforts for the florists' organization occurred during the 1965 Tournament of Roses Parade in Pasadena—a nationally televised event. Through PR work, the president of Florists' Transworld Delivery sat in the commentator's box and contributed his knowledge of flowers to the comments by John Forsythe and Betty White. The credit or "plug"? Identification of the president of FTD!

There are many ways PR can contribute to television programming; and just as every other media demands knowledge of its operation, so does television. You must know what makes good TV programming. The individual programs determine the format of a specific show, of course, but within the general framework of TV, there are specifics you must know about programming: what makes a good interview guest; what does an amateur guest do to look more professional on camera; what kind of props show best. TV is showmanship, and the more you know about the business, the better.

You can learn a lot about TV by watching it critically, not just for enjoyment or amusement. Why is one host better than another? Why is one newscaster more compelling and commanding than his competitor? Notice how little the pro uses his hands, except for a specific piece of business. Does he look at you? Does he smile? Yes. You feel that he's actually directing his conversation right at you.

These techniques are as true on your local station as on the major networks. Perhaps the network pro is more skilled —that's why he made it. But watch your local man or woman commentator closely; you'll learn from what they do —and shouldn't do!

For instance, the writer was working with a leading women's show commentator in Seattle, Washington. A guest was lined up for the show—an amateur in television, but an international expert in her field: botany and flower arranging. The guest, an articulate, vivacious woman, moved into the commentator's spotlight and took right over! The result was less than good programming because, no matter how fascinating an authority may be, on the medium of television it's the TV expert who must be in control.

In a case like this, what should PR do? Learn from it! Part of your job working with clients or people you place on TV is to advise them on their roles: what they should do and certainly what they should *not* do. The next appearance of the flower expert on another major TV show found her less demanding and more agreeable to watch and listen to.

The cardinal rule for working with TV people: *know what you're talking about.* Know the basics of the medium, know what you can offer. Is your material timely, newsy, does it have interesting aspects, is it good showmanship?

Network TV. Shows of a certain nature are always open to suggestions and ideas from public relations sources. Naturally, the nature of a show determines the scope of interest. A dramatic show would hardly be a logical spot to try to place a person or even plant an idea.

But programs such as "Today," "Tonight," the various personality variety shows and the big news programs are open and looking for ideas; each program has a special staff of researchers and writers who are constantly alert to unusual, timely possibilities for their particular show. To submit an idea for a show, you must contact the staff person responsible for a particular area—books, personalities, fashions, and so on. Unless you know the individual personally, it's better to send your idea, giving all the facts in brief outline form, and give him your phone number or contact referral. If the show is interested, you'll hear. If they're not, there's no way you can stimulate their interest, at least not with the same idea. Here's another basic to remember:

When you've tried to sell an idea or show,
Don't pester the staff for a "yes" or a "no!"

The *Publicity Record of New York* publishes a list of network and local New York television shows, their content and contacts for each. File cards are published regularly, and this is one way to build your own file, as well as check the constant changes that go on in this industry.

To approach any network TV show, be sure you:

—KNOW THE SHOW; KNOW IT'S FORMAT AND THE TYPE OF MATERIAL IT OFFERS ITS VIEWERS.
—ARE AN EXPERT ON WHAT YOU'RE OFFERING. You must sell your idea, so know your subject, whether it's an author, a jazz combo, the president of Hudson's Bay or the publisher of HARPER'S BAZAAR. Know your subject, know what the person can do or offer. Have an idea to sell.
—WRITE YOUR SUGGESTIONS IN OUTLINE FORM. Send them to the proper person or department. And spell everyone's name correctly!
—WAIT FOR AN ANSWER. If your idea is good and current enough, it will sell.

TV around the country. The opportunity for clever and resourceful public relations pros in the electronic media is growing all the time. Local programming is increasing, and local program directors, women's show directors, and news directors are open to sound, timely suggestions. Your people or product must have news value, must be timed right, must have a human interest aspect, and should have a semblance of showmanship.

Nearly every television station with live programming has specific departments and types of programs. Generally these include:

—*Children's programs.* There's Bozo in every big city—a charming clown, often with tears, who talks to and entertains little children. Sometimes Bozo is a tramp, a jolly fat man, or even a pretty young thing! But almost every sizeable station has a ringmaster for the kindergarten set, and he will welcome guests. Through the romping, singing and non-sense of these shows, smart PR people channel their new product news—if it's a chocolate milk product like Pet Milk's Big Shot. Guests who know how to talk to children can be interviewed by any number of Bozos throughout the country.

—*Civic programs.* Many TV stations have special civic or public service programs. Does your company or client have a message and personality with a *local* approach? An author-ity in an area that has strong local appeal is a sound sell. For instance, the "Make America Beautiful" campaign is primar-ily PR. Maybe your client is an expert nurseryman; he'd have a lot to say to any audience about ways to beautify a city. Maybe your client is a local brewery: what is it doing to beautify its city and state? There's probably a good spokes-man somewhere in the executive ranks who could speak with authority and effectiveness about the company's efforts.

—*Education programs.* These cover a wide range in many cities. The service or how-to aspect is important. Is there a safety official in your company's plant with an inter-esting story, a story with some general appeal? Have you an author to offer? Is your director of research an interesting man—can he talk about his work in packaging or product development in a way that's stimulating, provocative and in-formative? (Or will he freeze in front of a camera and be a dull addition to a program? If you even think so, forget it; you'll do yourself, your client and the station a disservice to present anyone who's a bomb. Nor will the station forget!)

—*Entertainment.* Guest appearance, audience participa-tion, panel and quiz shows fall in this category. The network shows in these groupings are open to PR people with person-alities and unusual people for their programs. On a local level, there is less availability of this type of show, although many of the major cities do have shows with some audience participation. People, products and ideas usually can be presented on shows of this type—the product mention or company identification is the extent of the credit.

—*Farm programs.* Stations in the farm belt of the country all have strong, large-audience farm programs. They're usually scheduled for very early morning or at noon, times when the farm audience is apt to be watching their sets. Most of these programs like to hear from PR people with timely news and information for their audiences. Your news, people or product must be right for this specific public—no ladies with fancy hats talking about hemlines!

—*Garden shows.* Some TV stations have regular garden shows for their audience, covering all aspects of plant care, gardening, lawns, and flowers. If your company or client has anything to offer this specific area, most of these programs are open to guests and news. Often, however, plant and garden show material is included in more general interest local programs, such as the women's shows.

—*News.* This is one constant in every station's programming! Every moment of every day marks another news event: every hour, someone or some event makes news. It could and often should be your client or company. The news may be of a national nature or strictly of local interest. TV newsmen are always open to tips on news and should be alerted to a planned event several days in advance, in writing. For instance, a ground-breaking ceremony for a multi-million-dollar plant, involving the board chairman of your company, the mayor and various councilmen, may not make network TV, but it's undoubtedly of enough interest locally to warrant a remote crew to cover the ceremony. (A remote crew means a cameraman and other TV technicians used away from the studio.) On the other hand, if your client, the Netherlands Flowerbulb Institute, arranges for the Dutch government to send a fresh, young Tulip Queen to tour America, her arrival at Kennedy International Airport *might* merit thirty seconds on a national newscast.

The PR pro in TV keeps the news department boys informed with professional memos on all newsworthy events. Keep those memos brief, succinct and factual. This is just another aspect of good reporting—part of your job as a PR pro.

—*Women's programs.* New York, Chicago, San Francisco—each has its own special women's programs. These major city shows usually are network or syndicated; they also are open to PR people with guest material or people of network caliber, such as personalities, authors, names in the news. Smaller local stations also have women's programs; there's hardly a station that doesn't offer some kind of live daytime programming directed to the distaff audience. Most of these programs cover a great variety of subject matter, ranging from cooking lessons to fashion tips. Whatever might be termed "women's interest" is a consideration on local programming. But it must be good. The requirements for local shows are becoming more demanding. You must have someone who's good on camera, who's good interview material. The subject must be newsy, timely. The better a showman you can offer, the better your reception will be next time around.

What can public relations offer television programs? Now you know the general areas of programming; naturally, as times change and new interest areas develop, different subjects will be given more attention.

Science and space shows have become weekly features, for example. The vital need for the PR expert is to keep abreast of news everywhere; know what's going on, know what's making news, what people are interested in learning more about. Then tailor your company or client's material to these interests.

The various techniques PR can use to work with the exciting and powerful medium of TV include:

—*Live appearances.* Offer interesting, provocative and articulate people for interviews, discussions and demonstrations. They must know what they're talking about. The more authoritative they are, the better . . . without being aggressive, of course!

—*Visuals.* Television is an alive, vibrant medium. What can your people *do*, what can they show, what can they explain *visually*? The more *meaningful action* you can inject, the better. This doesn't mean arm-waving or wasted movement; remember the top newscasters—they don't grimace, gesture. Visuals for amateurs (and your guests are likely to be television amateurs) should include props that can be explained, if possible—action blow-ups, equipment that moves, fashions that can be shown, something that can be touched, even if only a book. Keep it lively, offer something interesting visually.

—*TV kits.* These are complete features, with samples, visuals and script. A TV kit usually includes an actual sample of a product—can of applesauce, skein of yarn, a child's toy—along with other related visuals or props to tell an interesting story and to use in a demonstration. Horizontally printed matte-or dull-finish photographs and a script, with directions for the cameraman suggesting when the various visuals might be shown, complete the package. Professionally prepared, not-too-commercial TV kits often get a warm welcome on women's programs; they offer a service to viewers and are ready-to-air when the TV commentator receives them.

—*Newsreel footage.* News editors of stations throughout the country are interested in timely news events that have been professionally photographed and processed. For instance, during December, 1965, more than 200 stations presented a one-minute news film on American servicemen stationed in Europe receiving poinsettias from home. The entire film sequence was prepared and serviced by a public relations agency on behalf of a client, Interflora. The sequence was legitimate news and was produced by professional news photographers. The value to the client? Whenever anyone watching his local newscast saw the American army captain receiving flowers from home, this served as a reminder to the viewer: "*I* must order flowers!"

Several film companies specialize in making news film clips for distribution to television stations. If this is a new area for you, check with these experts and see how you can work with one of them for your company.

—*Films.* Many TV stations show films of timely nature which are not strictly news films. These films can run from five minutes to as long as twenty-five minutes, although the shorter films enjoy greater exposure. Films are an extremely effective way to tell your company's story or get your company's message across. Often this is done in an oblique way, with little commercial overtones. A travel tour of France, for instance, might mention the Champagne country—little more. Yet the vineyards of France could have been responsible for the travelogue.

A fashion film, describing what it means to be a model today, shows clothes designed with a du Pont fiber; the mannequins' slim figures are ascribed casually to Sego, the liquid diet food. But the impact of the film is *service*—how you can be a model, what you eat and wear.

Still another successful film clip tells the story of glass, or coffee or Cognac. Each offers the viewer a "new" story, an unusual angle or special interest feature.

Special interest films, stemming from public relations sources, usually are offered to program directors, women's program directors, special events directors and film directors of television stations, on an exclusive basis.

Educational television. Get up—it's sunrise and time for

your college credit course on television. Many educational channels now offer credit courses via TV and a great variety of essentially intellectually oriented programs during the course of the day. Also, there's a definite trend toward producing community service programing that is not offered by commercial TV. For example, the National Educational Television and Radio Center, NET, is vitally concerned with creating distinctive programs for its network. This includes the arts, humanities, social and physical sciences and children's programs.

The potential for public relations people working with educational television is more limited presently than opportunities with commercial TV. Programming, by its very nature, has primarily an educational orientation. Large corporations with ample budgets may underwrite the production costs for certain films, for example, and receive corporate identification both before and following the film or presentation. However, as a method for reaching a specific public with a specific message, educational TV is both less available and less effective than its commercial counterpart.

In the years ahead, however, this situation may reverse itself. As both industry and trade associations become more interested in education, perhaps public relations will work more closely and effectively with this important and intellectually stimulating aspect of TV.

Your future in TV is as exciting and wide open as the industry itself. This vital, of-the-moment medium is in its own adolescence, in terms of growth, and therefore opportunities for the PR pro with television knowledge are excellent.

Most of the job opportunities will be within two general categories. One, within companies and PR agencies with special departments for TV. As the industry itself grows the number of channels will increase; so will live programming at local levels. Both developments offer opportunities for PR pros with TV training, knowledge, and a flair for this particular brand of showmanship. Color, for instance, will become more important in future TV work; an artistic sense combined with a knowledge of how color responds to the camera will serve you well in PR oriented TV work.

Another major category for TV tomorrow will be within the public relations departments of stations. Today the major networks all have large PR departments; as local programming increases, local stations will have more jobs for public relations people. Whether you're working for a network or at a local level, your job will be similar: promoting and publicizing shows, programs and personalities scheduled for your station.

Educational TV will hold more jobs for PR people in the future: both for promoting ET channels, as well as working with agencies and companies to utilize any educational aspects.

Reviewing the basics again, you should:

—Know as much as possible about the medium. Watch it critically; take courses in it. Note the trends in programming.

—Read books about writing for TV; learn what on-camera demands are, what makes good programming and what does not.

—Apply your knowledge of photography to this living medium. Learn even more about color and photographing it.

Then, back to the fundamental precept of PR: apply your depth knowledge of your company or client to the demands of TV.

Good show!

9 PR on the Beam—
With Radio

You *can* take it with you, and literally millions of American's do, every hour of the day and night. Beaches, cars, parking lots, lobbies, beauty salons, offices, football stadiums—there's no place that modern radio isn't blaring or beating out its timely message.

More than half a century ago Guglielmo Marconi won the Nobel prize in physics for his work with electromagnetic waves or wireless telephony. His genius brought incredible new worlds of sound to humanity—a remarkable method of communicating that now pervades every moment of our lives. And radio is still growing.

Often the first thing one does on awakening is turn on the radio—what's the time and weather? And there's nothing unusual about someone walking down the street holding a transistor radio, listening intently to music, news or talk.

In 1966, there were more than 242,000,000 radio sets being used in this country; nearly every home has at least one working set, ranging from a tiny matchbox transistor to a handsome AM-FM console. According to *Broadcasting Yearbook*, more than *90 percent* of the entire population listens to the radio at least once a week, and 66 percent of the population makes it a daily habit.

During the past few years there has been a marked change in radio programming. The tempo of today is talk. Talk shows resound everywhere: interviews, conversations, soliloquies, visits, telephone-beep talks—talk, talk, talking of every manner and description has taken over the airwaves.

The talkathons are more than just hollow words. Good ideas, provocative conversational sessions are making more people than ever tune in their favorite station. Radio, today and tomorrow, offers tremendous opportunity for public relations activity. The effective use of words—getting a message across to a particular public—is a basic premise of PR. Radio, to the creative PR person, can be an excellent method of reaching a desired audience.

It's interesting that in the "age of television" radio broadcasting is bigger than ever. And this trend is growing: last year more than thirty-one million Americans bought radios —far more sets than were purchased the previous year.

The creative, knowledgeable PR person can work with this mighty medium in a number of ways. You start by listening. Hear what's being broadcast. Listen to the talk shows; find out what people want to hear, what they call the broadcasters about; discover what kind of conversations are being aired more than others. Listen at different hours of the day and night and learn all you can about this vital medium. Then you can offer ideas, people, programs and news events. But you must know how radio works and how you can work with it. Internally, radio functions much as television or newspapers do. There's a specific department for certain kinds of news and information. You must know where to deliver your idea or message, and the best form for it.

Here's a word of caution: the opportunities for PR in radio are vast, but the caliber of your material must be excellent. Competition for air time is stronger than ever, as more and more people, companies and organizations have increasingly more to say. Public service time is at a greater premium, for as our civilization becomes more complex, the areas of "public service" activities become broader.

Service is the key to getting radio time. A timely, interesting, newsworthy service approach is your password to getting your word out over the air. We live in a how-to world— what's it all about? If you can determine a *valid* how-to angle for your company's message or product, you probably can get it aired to the proper audience.

The first consideration for PR work with radio is to determine the public you want to reach. This is fundamental to all public relations activity—the premise applies to any PR effort, and it can't be repeated too often. When you've determined the public or audience you want to reach, inform, educate or influence, radio can be one of the methods.

Next step: learn about the various departments of a radio station and what kinds of programming each offers its listeners. One of the tools you'll find helpful is the *Working Press of the Nation's Radio and TV Directory.* This compendium of both television and radio station data is published annually, so you can be fairly certain the information is timely; you'll find this particularly helpful for checking who is responsible for a specific program or department, as well as facts about various programs, such as time, frequency and whether or not guests are welcome.

Program checklist for local radio. Most stations operate on a similar schedule. Programming starts early in the morning, often with a farm program or wake-up show of local origin. Programming is directed to various audiences during the day and into the night, offering broadcasts of special appeal to almost everyone, from children to sports fans. Here's a general category listing of the kinds of programming you'll find in just about every area of the country.

—*Children's programs.* Radio has its children's audience,

as does TV and the comics! Radio programs directed to children are apt to have a format created for children older than those TV aims at, but the best way to know is to listen. When this is impossible, write the MC of the show directly; he'll be glad to tell you what goes on during his program and whether he can use "outside" material—maybe yours! Typical radio programs for youngsters range from "Story Hours" without guests to "Teen Time" on KCKY in Coolidge, Arizona (host Jon Steele does welcome guests), or "Let's Dig This" with Tom Moore in Danville, Virginia, WDVA, a Sunday show also open to guests.

—*Civic programs.* Radio is still a crusading force in the world of communications, and civic programs rank high on the list of service broadcasting. Nearly every local station has some kind of civic program, often concerned with local questions and problems, but also open to discussions of greater scope, such as politics, perspectives, education and public opinion. Programs of this nature draw a definite audience—usually those of an intellectual nature, often of a certain economic status, and very often the more influential members of a community.

—*Entertainment.* "There's a gude time coming"—and Sir Walter Scott didn't even know about radio! Tune in any time of day, anywhere, and you'll find a radio program in the "good time" or entertainment category. Music, chatter, more music and, today, a lot more talk!

Maybe it's "Bandstand" on WFIX in Huntsville, the "Mitch Jordon Show" on KTYM in Inglewood, the "Western Show" on WCAZ in Carthage, the "Art Pallen Show" on KDKA in Pittsburgh—there's just "no business like show business!"

Some of the entertainment programs have guests, many have interesting features—it's up to you to find out and know what programming requirements are, and then you'll know if your material can be tailored for this type of radio.

—*Farm programs.* Just about every station in every state

has a program directed to the farm audience; it's usually on the air very early, at noon or late in the day, depending on the area of the country. These are chatty programs, with agricultural, conservation, 4-H livestock and county agent news presented. Often guests are welcome, guests with a definite farm-oriented message or point of view. If your client or company has something to say to this particular audience, you should be able to place ideas and people on these well-listened-to programs.

—*Garden programs.* Many smaller stations have garden shows, distinct from the farm programs. This is a different listening group—garden club ladies, green thumb experts, home owners with lawns and gardens. Guests with a garden message often can be scheduled, but they must know what they're talking about and have a special message to deliver.

—*News.* Every active station has live news programs, often scheduled several times during the day. Every kind of news is aired, from international reports to community projects. If PR is making a news show, it must be similar to any other medium: *it must be real news.* When you can tie in a local angle, so much the better. It must be presented in top professional radio-news form. Sometimes local news programs interview guests. If your client has an articulate, interesting person with a genuine news-oriented message, you probably can place him on news programs, even in the larger cities. To do so requires considerable advance work on your part. You must contact the news director, outline your guest's message, provide a profile of him and do a lot of careful follow-up work—confirmations, (with both the studio and the guest), making certain he's there on time and ready to go on the air. Being thorough is an important part of your work with radio stations in public relations.

—*Quiz shows.* Radio has its share of quiz programs, often audience call-in musical programs. Sometimes guests are welcome—depending on the specific program. Quiz shows by their nature offer some kind of prizes, and if your company has merchandise that's available as prize material, this can be another way to present your product to a particular public.

—*Religious programs.* Nearly every smaller station has one religious-oriented program, ranging from old-fashioned gospel hours to an "Ask the Pastor" program. Guests often are welcome; the public relations person involved with church programs, denominational causes, or youth groups can contribute to religious programs.

—*Safety programs.* Safety is a concern of everyone, and the many aspects of safety are the source of many good radio programs. Traffic, industry, home safety highways—even marine and surfers' information—merit broadcast time. Most of these programs are of a news nature, but occasionally a guest is welcomed into the safety lane. Does your company make motorboats? You must have a sound summertime message for the millions of boaters in America; the safety director of your company should have plenty to say.

—*Sports.* Sportscasters give their news and views from countless stations each day. Some shows interview guests, those with a definite sports-oriented story or news event. Maybe your company makes watches: is there a golfer who wears them or represents your company? If he's good enough, he can give hot golf tips, stance suggestions and fairway facts—as a representative of your watch company.

Women's programs. Radio programs for women are as ubiquitous and important as the women's page of a newspaper. Every station and every paper has one. Women's interests run the gamut, so your ability to place ideas, people, products or features on women's radio programs depends on how effective a public relations person you are.

Most women's programs are interested in guests—guests who really have something to offer. This is a highly competitive area, so your guest or message must be that much better than the next PR person's.

Remember, service is the key; however your guest or information can improve, enlighten or enlarge the worlds of the women who listen to radio will determine how successful that guest is. He or she must have something to say and say it well with little or no commercial overtones. Identification of a company or product should suffice for commercial credit on any radio program.

Another helpful way to learn about the programming from any given area of the country is to order out-of-town newspapers and study the radio listings. When you have questions about a particular listing, a letter directed to that program usually will get a response. Radio people are like most other people: they respond to an interest in *them* and what they're doing.

Material for broadcast. When you've determined what kind of programs are on the air, then decide if your company or client has a legitimate message for the audience who listens to any given program. Is it

—News?   23347
—Timely?
—On target—both for the radio station and your company?

If so, what next? Prepare your material properly for a particular kind of program or broadcast. A farm audience gets one kind of copy, a women's program another, news still another. You must learn what is good radio copy and what isn't. Take a course in radio writing; work part time at a studio—do any kind of work, type, answer phones, write continuity (if you can), but learn everything you can about the medium. Learn it from books, if necessary, but work at it!

To show you how radio copy differs in form from newspa-

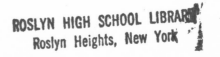

per releases, here are examples on the same topic, directed to
the different media. Jan Aaron, a bright, young account executive in a New York agency which represents the Government of India Tourist Office, is a versatile writer who knows
how to adapt her subject to the demands of a given medium.
Here's how she handled a radio script on Kashmir, prepared
for women's commentators:

READING TIME: 1:45

CONSIDER KASHMIR THIS YEAR

How about a vacation in Paradise? Before you
settle for the same place with high prices and
hordes of people, let me tell you about one of the
oldest resorts around. Strangely enough, it's one of
the least discovered retreats in the world.

This lotus-eater's paradise is Kashmir—a two-
hour flight from Delhi, India's capital. Vacationers
have been going there for 400 years, starting with
the great Eastern Emperors. Today, tourists can
live in Oriental splendor . . .

The identical subject was released to travel editors on the
nation's newspapers. Here's how this copy read:

FROM: EG&A INTERNATIONAL, INC.
         640 Fifth Avenue, New York 10019
         JUdson 2-7540 (Jan Aaron)
FOR: GOVERNMENT OF INDIA TOURIST OFFICE
                              Exclusive in Your City
                              FOR IMMEDIATE RELEASE

KASHMIR: RESORT OF MANY SPLENDORED CHARMS

A lake with jade green waters and a "meadow of gold" are
only two of the natural wonders to be seen in Kashmir. However, visitors to India's beautiful resort do not have to be
content with scenic splendor alone. They can play golf, tennis, swim or water ski in this Himalayan retreat, just two
hours from Delhi by plane.

Radio writing is strictly second person. Occasionally it invokes the first person for an opinion or point of view. But *you* are the key element in conversation for radio.

Here's a quick test to try the broadcast ability of your copy: *read it out loud.* Does it sound easy, natural? You're writing for the *ear,* remember. Read it aloud again—then go rewrite it!

A helpful handbook for publicity people offered by the National Association of Broadcasters is called *"If You Want Air Time."* Among the points it makes are:

"Competition is tough. To enhance your own chances of getting public service time, make certain that:

Your message is important and of widespread interest. It is presented in the best possible form."

The resourceful public relations man will know what's being broadcast, as well as the best method of presenting material to broadcasters.

One creative and effective approach for public service time was conceived by Wayne Pennington, a PR consultant to Bayer Aspirin and its parent company, Sterling Drug.

THE PROBLEM:	Reach the vast public concerned with health and good health measures.
THE MESSAGE:	Underscore public recognition of Sterling Drug, makers of Bayer Aspirin, as one of the most reputable, authoritative sources of information about health (and incidentally, health-oriented products!).
THE METHOD:	*Medicine, '66*—a provocative, informative documented series of interviews on vital health questions, with physicians and qualified professionals.
THE RESULT:	More than 1,000 radio stations used this public service, electrically transcribed series during 1966, and requested a requel.

This particular series is cited because it's an excellent example of creative public relations at work. Here's the story: Wayne Pennington, account supervisor for Sterling Drug, mapped out a complete public service program for the drug company, based on the requisites of radio needs: *newsworthy copy, timely information,* and *directly on target*—both for the stations and his company.

First of all, 3,000 radio stations were surveyed for their interest in the initial series. The stations were offered the non-commercial electrical transcription album series on an exclusive basis. More than 1,000 stations throughout the country requested the series and reported actual air time usage later. (This is a high ratio of usage.)

Each segment on *Medicine '66* was about three and one half minutes of short, concise and fascinating discussion on such subjects as health check-ups, heart disease and cholesterol, the common cold, headaches. Each subject was handled in interview form by a professional announcer and a physician noted in that specific health area.

At the open and close of each 3½-minute session the "science reporter" or announcer referred to *"Medicine '66,* a public service of Sterling Drug Company" or, in some instances, "the Bayer Company." That was the extent of commercial credit or identification; the interviews covered questions a listener would want to know, such as how often one should have a physical check-up, why you should go to a doctor even when you feel well, and what kind of ailments are detected through routine checks. The actual interviews were generic, educational and highly factual. PR effectively at work on the air!

Mr. Pennington, who speaks with quiet, Southern-bred authority, gives these suggestions to other public service features for broadcasting:

"If you plan a series like this, be sure to get the best production facilities available. You'll be working with amateurs, as far as interviews are concerned. But the result must be professional. So budget for the best in the business. When we went on remotes—that's the best way to interview busy professional people—the producer had a sound engineer with him.

Talking to people in their own office or home is better. You get more natural sounding conversation. Remember, people are busy; you've got to work at *their* convenience—make your arrangements to suit them."

Mr. Pennington also mentioned the additional public relations value of *Medicine '66* to his company: it was used as a promotional piece to important stores selling Sterling products to underscore the "good citizen" role of the company. All the physicians interviewed received an album, along with a personal letter from a key executive of the company. Also, the series was publicized in the broadcast trade publications.

Working with the networks. Turn on your radio any weekend, anywhere in the country, and tune in one of the major network radio programs that command top listening audiences right around the clock. CBS radio has its *Weekend Dimension,* and NBC's *Monitor* is familiar listening fare.

Do public relations people work with the writers of these top-notch programs?

"Of course we do. It's my personal opinion that PR people are vital to us," Cappy Petrasch, feature editor for NBC *Monitor,* spoke unequivocally in her cozy book- and picture-filled office high in the NBC towers of Manhattan.

"Basically, we get leads and stories from several sources. Our own news correspondents, free-lancers, and from NBC affiliates here and abroad. We get ideas from newspapers and periodicals—and a lot of good leads come from publicists. We need their help. The good ones do a real job to help us cover the volume of material we must have for good programming."

She went on to say: "Here's how the good ones work: they

call with an angle. You know—something really interesting. For instance, the client might be a clothing manufacturer, but he's also the world's greatest humming bird authority. *That's* interesting! Or maybe it's a show personality who has something to say. He *thinks*. Maybe it's about music, theatre, yoga. But something that's off-beat—the world loves the off-beat, you know. Good publicists are honest, too. We get to depend on their honesty. They know a good story, and what we'll use."

This young woman, responsible for many of the timely features on *Monitor* radio, offers good advice to young people considering public relations:

"The other day a man called and said he didn't listen to the show but wondered what kind of material we could use. We explained because he might have had something worthwhile. But that's irritating.

"Then the other day another publicity man called to offer a 'white hunter' for an interview. I was curious, so asked him for a biography. He sent a commercial sales brochure. We had to call and request a real biography. You know what? The PR fellow suggested we call the 'white hunter' and get it! I guess he went hunting," she added quietly.

Miss Petrasch believes that honesty, hard work and good writing are musts for PR people who want to work with any broadcast media. A second language is an advantage, she believes. "Too few Americans can speak anything but English. In all communications—particularly radio, both AM and FM, a second language will be an asset in the future."

What other experts say. A special clinic on radio and TV broadcasting was held in February, 1966, by the Public Relations Society of America. Three network news professionals headed the panel entitled, "What the Networks and Stations Want from Public Relations People." The men were George Heinemann, Public Affairs Manager, NBC-TV News; Zeke Segel, National Assignment Manager, CBS-TV; and Ed Silverman, News Director, ABC-TV News. Their suggestions, though reflecting a TV expert's view, are equally applicable to radio. They include:

1. Don't be heavy handed in trying to get an on-the-air plug. If there's a real story, the person or company who sets up the story is entitled to mention, but don't try and force it on a reporter.

2. Affiliate stations around the country usually alert network news departments about events in their local areas. If the PR man can get a local station to cover such an event, there's a good chance that the station will suggest it to the network.

A final quote from the PRSA "Memo" (March 1966) bears repeating. The newsmen told the Clinic:

"It used to be that a story suggested by a PR representative was immediately tossed out. That no longer holds true. We do need you, and we can work together."

How well you work together will depend on you. You must know what's being broadcast, what the programers are open to in terms of ideas. You must know your company with the authority of an expert, and your material or representative must reflect that knowledge. Your material must be presented in top professional form.

Tomorrow's radio will be available to the public relations pro—the fellow who has something to offer, knows how to say it, and says it at the right time.

As one PR expert says, "Sure we work with radio, whenever we can. It's show business—with a twist."

A clever "twist," with the positive public relations result for everyone concerned, was reported by *Women's Wear Daily* (July 22, 1966) during a major airline strike:

"With the airline strike leaving hundreds of stewardesses in San Francisco with an abundance of time and diminishing financial resources, Bay Area disk jockeys are jumping on the rescue bandwagon. KSFO's Dan Sorkin has his "save our stewardesses" clearing agency for supper dates and KNRB's Frank Dill has declared July 24-30 as "take a stewardess to lunch" . . . and will begin it Monday by taking 25 of them from United to the Golden Pavilion."

Good PR for the radio stations, the restaurant—and did it just *happen* to be United? Not with an alert PR department serving an idea "with a twist"!

The world of broadcasting is ready and willing for good PR material. Are *you* ready?

10 Four Major Work Areas—
Take Your Choice

When you start job-hunting in the public relations field, you'll find that there are four major areas to consider. The areas are company public relations, where you'll become a member of the public relations department of one firm; agency jobs where you'll work with several different clients; trade associations where you'll represent a number of organizations within a specific industry; and non-profit PR where you'll be on the staff of a social, religious, service, or governmental organization. There are good jobs in all four areas but each has distinct advantages and disadvantages.

Let's look at each of these four in detail so you can aim for the area which best suits your talents, goals and personality. A good way to define your own objectives is to think long thoughts about where you'd like to be five years from now . . . the town, the job, the work which would be most rewarding to you. Ask yourself, "What type of life and work would I want more than any other?" Then shoot for that.

Company public relations. Today, there are about fifty thousand people in the United States in public relations work. This figure is based on an estimate by the U.S. Department of Labor, reflecting the U.S. Census Bureau estimate of 60,000. It's a little higher than John W. Hill's estimate of 40,000 cited in his book *The Making of a Public Relations Man* and a little under *PR Reporter's* researched figure of 57,000. Company public relations jobs, now a big portion of this total, will offer even more job opportunities in the future.

Today, thousands of firms have either a public relations department or at least one public relations expert. A survey by PR Publishing Co., Inc., taken among major non-government organizations in the United States and Canada, showed that most corporations with more than $6 million in sales and at least 500 employees are involved in a public relations program of some type. The same study revealed that these organizations were spending about $500,000,000 on public relations each year.

There are job opportunities in all types of corporations ranging from banks, breweries and paper mills to perfume manufacturers. If you have a strong interest in a certain industry, you'll be able to find a PR job in that field.

If you decide on a company PR job, you'll have a wide choice of where you'll live and work, since corporate jobs exist in most sections of the nation. Generally, you'll find the company's public relations department is located in its main headquarters or "home office," but because corporations are located in all parts of the country, the PR jobs are too. New York City is the headquarters city for many of the giant business enterprises so you'll find more company jobs there, but you'll also find them in smaller cities. An indicator of the geographic spread is the fact that the Public Relations Society of America now has fifty-five chapters spread from Hawaii to Niagara Falls, up through New England and down to Baton Rouge. Each chapter has more members in corporate jobs than any other type, so you have at least fifty-five different places to live!

Now, suppose you've picked your very favorite area and found the type of company which fascinates you; what will your job be like?

First of all, you'll probably work in a fairly small department which is more fun and less formal than a big one. The PR Publishing Company study showed in a survey of 10,000 firms that 52 percent have fewer than four PR people and 91 percent fewer than fifteen. You'll know everyone quickly, say "hi" on a first-name basis, and you'll work without a lot of the red tape which binds many big PR departments.

Then you'll probably work in an office which has the sign "Public Relations Department" on the door. Sometimes, the functions of public relations and advertising are combined in one department and occasionally both PR and advertising come under the marketing department.

Before you get your new job, you'll be interviewed by the public relations director, of course, and you probably will also be interviewed by the Personnel Department, as part of the company's regular hiring procedure.

When you're officially on the payroll, you'll become eligible for all the employee benefits which your company offers —sick pay, paid vacation, group insurance, hospitalization and participation in any pension or incentive plans which are offered. All this talk about protection, pensions and security may seem dreary to you now, but these benefits are there to give you greater peace of mind and security in the future. They also add to your salary, although you never see it reflected in your paycheck; listen to the explanations and study the material you'll receive—it's worth money to you!

You'll find that company jobs offer far greater security and "fringe" benefits than any other PR area. Agencies, associations and non-profit groups really can't compete. You'll also find that you're likely to have more job security working for a company.

Salaries for beginners in corporate public relations vary

with the area. They're generally higher in the East than in the Midwest and West, and also somewhat higher North than South. Usually, the larger the town, the higher the salary scale. But you can plan on a starting rate of about $5,000 to $7,000 a year. From there, you can climb as high as $70,-000 a year as director of public relations for a giant company! Of course, most company directors don't command that figure. Analysis of an American University survey shows that the average salary for public relations directors of major corporations is $31,642 a year. But, to give you more about this "typical" PR director, another study reports that he's forty-four years old, a college graduate, has been with his present organization eight years but has had fourteen years in public relations or a related field; he belongs to his local country club and owns two cars.

Functions and structure of corporate public relations departments vary. A few giant enterprises have PR staffs of several hundred people working from offices all over the world. Du Pont de Nemours Company, Inc., employs more than three hundred people in its far-flung PR operation, with particular groups assigned to specific products. However, most departments are much smaller with a less complex structure.

In a medium-sized corporation, the PR department will probably handle a wide range of assignments—product promotion, employee relations, community relations, stockholder relations, and it may even be involved in labor relations and customer relations. Where does the newcomer fit into this picture? Very often, the beginner will start his career working on the company newspaper, reporting directly to the editor.

This is a great place to learn all there is to know about the company and to sharpen a variety of skills. Company publications run the gamut from glossy, full-color monthly magazines to simple newspapers published once or twice a month; the assistant on the company publication, plain or fancy, will be learning something new every day.

Suppose you start in this job; what will you be doing? Realistically, you'll get the "dirty work" at first. You'll cover simple stories which the editor can't find time to do. You'll do a lot of "leg work"—running around the plant or office getting stories approved, handling simple interviews and photo assignments and maybe fetching coffee for everyone in the department. You'll proofread, learn a lot about typography, layout, make-up and other phases of the graphic arts; you may be in for some after-hours work, since most company publications cover evening and weekend events—the bowling league banquet, annual Christmas party, speeches by top executives before civic groups and similar company affairs.

Whether you start your corporate career as an assistant on the publication staff or simply as a trainee in the PR department, you'll meet people from all levels of management and from all departments in the company; you'll learn something about every function, from production to accounting, from sales to research. As a trainee or junior writer in the department, you'll have a wide range of assignments, too. One week you may be doing research for a soon-to-be-published corporate history . . . the next week, writing and laying out an employee handbook. Then you may work on the first draft of a film on plant safety. Soon you'll feel that you're an important part of the company. This feeling of "belonging," of being an "insider," is something you won't find if you work for an agency or a trade association. If this feeling is important to your personal happiness, you'll do well to look for a corporate job.

However, there are disadvantages to the corporate job. Salaries are somewhat lower than those at agencies and there is a "sameness" about the work. An editor of a company publication once said that publishing the magazine was "just like doing the dishes—you finish one issue and it's time to start another."

To sum it up, corporate jobs offer greater job security, participation in important benefit programs and a feeling of "belonging"; agency jobs offer slightly more salary and more variety but also mean more pressure and less security.

Public relations agencies. Denny Griswold, editor and publisher of *Public Relations News,* estimates that there are some fifteen hundred public relations counseling firms in the United States and predicts that by that magic year 1984: "The corps of PR professionals will expand to more than 300,000 . . . counseling firms will number 5,000 . . . budgets will reach a whopping $10 billion annually."

Mrs. Griswold is a veteran of the business and has long been active in professional activities. If her estimate is correct, the public relations counseling field will expand more than 300 percent in the next seventeen years, so job opportunities here for you could hardly be brighter.

Before taking a closer look at this area, it might be well to review the terms. "Public relations agency," "publc relations consultants" and "public relations counselors" are all phrases used to describe the same type of business—the independent firm of public relations specialists which serves several different client organizations. These firms are structured much like a law firm and operate on similar lines.

A public relations agency can be a "one-man show" or a large, substantial firm employing up to two or three hundred people. The agency really has only one thing to "sell," the talent of its people. It "sells" this talent much the way a law firm does—on the basis of charges for time. Of course, methods of charging for time vary. Some agencies charge clients a flat monthly retainer fee, and no matter how much or how little time is spent on the client's behalf, the fee remains the same. Others charge by the hour or day. Members

PHILADELPHIA

PROMOTION

STORE TIE-INS—PR activity coordinated with store promotions is one facet of effective public relations programs. Here, Northeast Airlines offers a "Yellowbird Honeymoon" to bridal customers of a large Philadelphia store. This page was compiled for a report to the client by the PR firm; circled areas denote the promotion posters used in various departments.

OBJECTIVES

Motorcycle Riding Is Fun

Solid Citizens Are Riders

Economical & Practical Transportation

Health Benefits

Safety Education

REPORTING PR ACTIVITY—Public relations agencies must make reports on activity to their clients, to explain what's happening and sometimes *why* it's happening. To improve the image of motorcyclists, a PR firm was retained by an association of manufacturers of cycles and motor bikes. This page, from a regular report to association members, explains the premise of the PR campaign.

MOTORCYCLES MEAN BIG BUSINESS—the boom in motorcycle sales warranted editorial space in major magazines. The PR man's job is to bring the news value of a story to the attention of top publications. He contacts the publication with an idea, provides photos, information and background material. Here are examples from a report to motorcycle association members of news stories that made the "big time."

WHITE COLLAR RIDERS

"SET-UP" PHOTOS AND THEIR USE—the association PR man noted more businessmen ride motorcycles today. A good picture story idea! He contacted a photo feature syndicate, lined up real cycle riders, even cleared traffic for the photographer. Result? The four-picture insert shows how a newspaper used the syndicated material, publicizing the new, positive image.

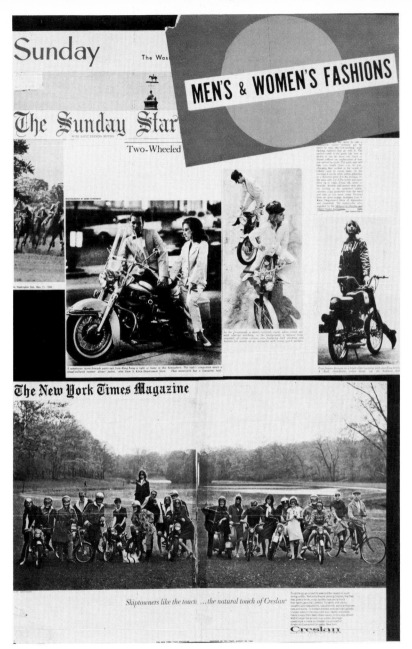

FASHIONS ON A BIKE—to underscore the improved image of motorcycle riders, the trade association PR firm worked with leading fashion designers in special photography sessions. This is another aspect of touching all elements in a well-planned public relations campaign.

TALKING TO TEENS—PR often works with media directed to a
certain market or public. Here a handknit suit was created for
AMERICAN GIRL by Bernat Yarns; instructions for knitting were
offered through the magazine, and the issue was merchandized or
promoted in yarn shops throughout the country. Another phase of
PR in fashion!

SAY IT WITH FLOWERS—in the nation's news syndicates. Here, a syndicated column suggests using Florists' Transworld Delivery services for remembering special dates. This page was part of a report to the FTD client by its PR agency.

ONE GOOD STORY—may mean many placements across the country. Here a pretty girl touches a replica of an ancient English kissing ball; the copy tells about this traditional use of fresh flowers—and reminds readers the unusual floral arrangement is available today through FTD florists. A good journalistic writing style is important to a publicist doing PR work.

KNBC-TV
Los Angeles

KPIX-TV
San Francisco

WRC-TV
Washington

KVOA-TV
Tucson

WMAL-TV
Washington

KTVW-TV
Tacoma

TV IS A VITAL PART OF PR PLANNING—placing people on behalf of your company or client on various television programs is another facet of public relations activity. This client-report page shows floral arranging experts appearing on TV shows in different cities. Working with all media is the PR man's job.

INTERNATIONAL PR AT WORK—an English and Japanese sign welcomes 55 Tokyo florists who toured this country as part of an international public relations program for the world-wide flowers-by-wire organization. This photo was serviced to the floral trade publications, as part of the trade or business-oriented PR program for the client.

PR ON CAMERA!—the writer advises a model how to hold a new cosmetic for the camera. The publicist and the photographer had to work between "takes" during a film sequence for a TV commercial to get a series of "how-to-apply" photographs for newspaper editorial use.

FASHIONS ON PARADE—part of fashion public relations work is the excitement of arranging fashion shows for the press and retailers, often in exotic settings. Here Bernat Yarns show new designs for knitters during a special luncheon at Manhattan's towering Rainbow Room—65 floors above the city streets.

NAMES ARE NEWS!—HARPER'S BAZAAR publisher, William Fine (third from left), holds the spotlight during a session of Johnny Carson's network "Tonight" show (NBC-TV). Also on stage are Jack Haskell, Stephanie Powers and Mr. Carson. Mr. Fine talked about the fashion magazine's 100th anniversary celebration.

INTERNATIONAL NEWS—Holland's Parliament in The Hague is traditionally opened by the Queen, who arrives in the royal Golden Coach. It is an event publicized by the PR firm promoting travel to The Netherlands. The pomp and splendor of this occasion has unique news value to travel editors in America.

FIRST IN FASHION—Nancy White (center), editor of HARPER'S BAZAAR, whets American fashion palettes with news of the French couturier collections following showings she viewed in Paris. Barbara Walters and Hugh Downs of NBC-TV's "Today" show listen to the fashion authority's report—a public relations' appearance to personalize the image of this top fashion magazine.

PR PAYS OFF—to the winner and the company! During the New York World's Fair the Pet Milk Company exhibit included a column of cash, to be awarded to the closest guesser of the amount. The winner receives her prize from PR Director Arthur E. Wright, Jr., while Account Executive Martha Olson and other officials look on. Millions looked at the Pet exhibit—more than a million guessed at the amount and countless customers remembered Pet products as a result of this unusual PR stunt.

CHILDREN'S TV SHOWS—a natural for specialized PR activity. The writer presents Jerry Wheeler (Lorenzo the Clown, a television favorite in Baltimore) with a floral soda, just for fun! Youngsters see fresh flowers in new arrangements, they learn about flowers from an FTD spokeswoman—and florists enjoy a novel approach to showing and selling their product.

BEAUTY AT BEST—models pose for publicity shots, showing Coty Originals make-up being applied. Publicity is part of public relations planning and good "action" photographs could mean editorial placement in cities where the products are sold.

PR HELPS HUNT FOR STEWARDESSES—when Northeast Airlines conducted a stewardess recruitment drive, public relations activity supported the program. Press interviews with veteran stewardesses were set up in several Eastern seaboard cities; these girls appeared on TV, talked with newspaper editors and radio commentators—extolling the positives of being a high flying Yellowbird hostess!

FOOD FOR THOUGHT—the food industry uses public relations activity extensively—from big baking contests to creating new recipes for publicizing food products. Here the Lipton Kitchens suggest a savory stuffing for salmon (made with Thousand Island dressing!). All arrangements for this visual feast were prepared by the PR people, from the baking to pouring tea into carefully chosen china cups.

HARDY CANADIAN VOYAGEURS paddled to New York from Montreal in August, 1966 to lay a wreath at the base of the Statue of Liberty honoring the Statue as a symbol of welcome to foreign peoples. On May 24, in honor of Canada's Centennial, these same 72 men in 12 canoes were to travel 3,283 miles of lake and river retracing the fur trade route begun 300 years ago.

of the staff keep time records (lawyers do the same thing) and, at the end of the month, the client is billed for all the time which has been spent on his affairs with the billing based on a known hourly or daily rate or rates. Other agencies use a combination of the two systems, charging a monthly retainer for counsel by the principals, plus time charges for staff work.

Public relations counselors are bound by many of the same ethical standards which guide legal counselors: they cannot represent conflicting interests or use confidential information gained in work with client companies for their own selfish interests. And, like lawyers, the public relations consultants usually maintain offices separate from any client and are not considered as employees of the client company, but as "outside experts."

If you think you would like a PR agency job, you'd better like urban living, for this is usually a "big town" operation. In fact, almost 50 percent of the nation's 1,700 agencies are located in New York.

There are two reasons for this. The first is very basic—money! There just aren't enough large firms, associations and organizations in a medium-sized or small town to support an independent counseling firm. The second reason is that the communications media are centered in major population centers. So if you prefer to work in an agency, head for New York, Chicago, Los Angeles, Boston, St. Louis or Philadelphia or some other large city.

Who uses public relations counselors and why? There are many answers, and all of them right. An individual may have one or more so-called public relations counselors on his payroll to get personal publicity. This is particularly true in Hollywood and New York. Clients are usually entertainers, and counselors are press agents (sometimes called "flacks"). The job? Get as many items as possible in the gossip column, showbiz publications and magazines. In New York, press agents may specialize in column contacts—their major job is to get clients mentioned in syndicated columns. Other press agents in the world of entertainment handle both individual stars and Broadway shows. If their show is a "turkey" and closes after two performances, they look for "another opening, another show."

Other individuals who may hire a press agent to gain personal publicity are society people, members of the "jet set," fashion designers, politicians, and restaurateurs.

However, this show business, society type of promotion is a fringe area of public relations, with few opportunities for beginners. It's glamorous—but sometimes shabby. Press agents in this field often are one-man operators who may "operate out of a phone booth"; in other words, most of them don't have an office, much less a staff. They rely on their personal contacts and personal hard work to earn a living.

PR's big business. The real volume of business for the public relations agency is in serving corporations, associations and governments. For the large agencies, this type of work can result in billings of as much as $4 million a year. Advertising agency billings may run into multimillions, but the two figures aren't comparable. Ad agency billings include the money used to *buy* time and space for a client. PR agencies sell only *service,* remember.

It has been estimated that 50 percent of all major corporations use PR counsel regularly and another 13 percent use outside firms occasionally.

To observers, there sometimes seems to be a conflict between a corporation's own PR department and outside counsel, but a report from the National Industrial Conference Board in 1965 showed that more companies with fully staffed PR departments use outside counsel than companies with no PR unit. Very often, the PR agency is hired by the corporate PR director, with management approval, and reports to the director on day-to-day matters. The agency is not in competition with the internal staff but rather strengthens it and supports its efforts through extra talent, time and experience.

Agency assignments for its clients run the gamut from complete public relations programming to specific, one-shot assignments. In some cases, an agency will concentrate on product promotion, on financial relations or on contacts with national media. In others, it will be responsible for all these assignments and many more.

The scope of the work performed by the agency generally is outlined in a written program prepared after research and consultation between the agency and client. Periodic progress reports are made to the client, and it's usual to have regular reviews or presentations given by the agency to the client to show how time and money are being spent and what results are achieved. These annual or semi-annual reports often are accompanied by a proposed new program for the next six months or year which the client can approve, reject or modify.

Many respected agencies have clients with whom they've worked for ten, fifteen or even twenty years; any working arrangement between counsel and client is subject to termination by either party, however, usually, upon thirty, sixty or ninety days written notice. This makes life in the agency business more precarious and tense than that in a corporation. Suppose you're the newest member of a medium-sized agency with annual billings of, say, $700,000. One of your major accounts or clients is a food company for which you carry out a $100,000 program each year. Suddenly, the management of your company decides to sell out to a much bigger food enterprise. Although you've done a great job, your agency drops about 15 percent of its total income almost overnight. Very often, the management of your agency has no choice but to cut back on expenses to compensate for this loss in revenue; since you're the last one hired, you're likely to be the first one fired. By the nature of the PR business, you can't count on job security; also, since agencies are really small enterprises in terms of staff, income and assets, many cannot support costly benefit programs—retirement incomes, guaranteed raises, full insurance coverage, overtime payments or even sick pay for extended illnesses. So if you're the security type, a PR agency may not be for you.

Several bright advantages offset the risks of the agency business, however. First, there's money. Generally, you'll find the starting salaries are somewhat higher than they are in any of the other major sectors of PR—corporate, association or non-profit jobs. Almost as important is excitement. If you enjoy change and challenge, the agency life can be highly satisfying, since work involves many different clients with many different problems to solve. Each working day will be somewhat different, with surprising new developments—both good and bad. Finally, experience. You'll cram more work experience into less time in an agency than in most other fields. You'll be working on four or five accounts in one year and you'll know something about each business when the year is over.

What's the secret of success in agency work? You'll need energy, ability to think clearly, ingenuity and the integrity required to succeed in other fields of public relations. But you'll also need a high degree of flexibility—the ability to jump intellectually from one problem to another, from one assignment to another, from contacts with different personalities in different fields.

Trade associations. Everyone wants to be in the act! Social critics claim that Americans are the world's greatest joiners—eager to belong to organized groups, attend meetings and participate in any number of clubs, lodges, societies and organizations. Perhaps this has contributed to the growth of associations. Today, there are at least thirteen thousand recognized trade, business, professional and commercial organizations in this country, and two thousand are nationwide in scope.

Think of almost any type of business, trade, art, profession, hobby or field of study, and you'll find that its followers are organized into an association. A quick way to survey the field is by looking through the *Encyclopedia of Associations* published by Gale Research Company. Pick a page at random, and you can find such listings as "National Horse Show Association of America," "International Jugglers' Association" and the "International Kitefliers Association." Believe it or not, there's even a trade association for trade associations —the American Society of Association Executives, headquartered in Washington, D.C., with a membership of 2,000 and a paid staff of twelve!

The association field is a good one for the public relations job-hunter, since the promotion and public relations function is very often one of the major jobs of the organization. Other functions commonly assigned to a business, professional, trade or commercial association are research, establishment and enforcement of standards and procedures, preparation and dissemination of technical information, and government contacts, including review of proposed legislation which might affect the group. Often the association also will provide members with training information, sales promotion guides, market studies, and will usually plan and arrange for one or more national meetings or conventions each year.

As a member of an association PR staff, you'll be involved in all of these activities on behalf of the members. You'll also work on a most important job—member relations, which includes projects to enroll new members and encourage maximum participation in association affairs. Part of your job will be keeping members informed on "what you've done for them lately."

Your job will have some of the advantages and disadvantages of both the corporate and agency fields. Like the corporate PR staffer, you'll be working 100 percent of your time for one organization, and you'll have some of the security and employee benefits which corporations offer. But like the agency field, you do face a more risky future. Association life can be plagued with internal politics, and the public relations department can be endangered by a sudden change in administration. Just as an agency can lose a big account, an association can suddenly lose a big group of members. This shock will almost surely be reflected in a reduced budget and reduced payroll so that you, the newcomer, may be out through no fault of your own. Associations generally are financed in one of three ways: through flat membership dues, through contributions based on sales or production, and by a combination of these two systems. You can understand that any drop in membership, a deep and sudden dip in sales or production spells almost instant retrenchment for the association management.

One advantage which trade association PR people have over corporate staffs is that getting publicity for a service or product which doesn't have a brand name is far easier. Many editors, program managers and directors shy away from brand-name identification but will welcome promotion under a generic name.

You'll find more trade association PR opportunities in New York and Washington than any other cities, since there are many associations headquartered in these two cities. But you don't have to live on the Eastern seaboard to work in this field. "Home town" for an association may be Chicago, Detroit, St. Louis, Los Angeles, San Francisco—almost any major city.

Non-profit organizations. The fourth major area for public relations practitioners is the "non-profit" field. This encompassing title covers the widest possible range of organizations and enterprises. It's a huge category and still growing. The non-profit designation fits such organizations as government agencies at every level—national, state, county, city and town; social agencies; health and welfare groups; educational institutions; charity groups; religious groups; and youth groups.

As a nation, we're showing increasing concern with the welfare of all our citizens. We spend more and more money, increasingly more time and talent to improve the lot of people through better education, better health and more economic security. Every campaign devoted to a "cause"—from President Lyndon Johnson's massive "Great Society" program to your home-town United Fund drive—must have public understanding and support if it's to succeed. To win these, sound public relations programming is required. This field is wide open to you who prefer working with a dedication or altruistic purpose.

Although these are jobs with "non-profit" groups, many can offer very comfortable salaries, great prestige and security. In the government service, for example, you'll find jobs within civil service ranks. Many of these offer not only good benefits and job security but also excitement and travel. The Defense Department, State Department and groups such as NASA and the United States Information Agency all employ PR people.

In this non-profit field, you'll use the same skills and techniques you would use in a corporate or agency job but you may thrill to the knowledge that you're not just contributing to the balance sheet of a business but to the well-being of a group of needy people or to the advancement of a science or art.

Each of the basic four major fields of public relations—

corporate, agency, associations and non-profit—offers pluses and potential to the PR aspirant. You begin with one basic; become a good generalist. Then listen to what experts in specific areas have to say. That's next on your journey and agenda.

11 Specialists Speak Out

First a generalist, then a specialist. It must be in that order.

Science public relations. Public relations has its specialists, but these experts are men and women who know the
rudiments of sound, general PR activity. The first of the
specialty areas is science. A lead article in *Life* during
August, 1966, written by the magazine's Science Editor, Al-
bert Rosenfeld, capsules the spirit of the world science today
and what it means. In this provocative column he says:

Science Is Where the Action Is

Science has already transformed our physical environment
quite radically and will do so even more as we learn to ma-
nipulate electrons, atoms, and molecules in ever more sophisticated ways, and as we extend our explorations into the
bottoms of oceans and out to the stars and planets. But the
most striking transformations will be in man himself.

We will, before too much longer, be able to control our
own physiology, including our brains; to reproduce without
the benefit of sex; to direct the heredity of individuals as well
as the evolution of the race. It would be hard to exaggerate

the sweeping nature of the implications for human societies and for fundamental human values . . .

I do suggest that writers accept and deal with science—not as a separate entity but as a permanent and powerful force that inescapably permeates our entire cultural atmosphere, affecting the everyday lives of all of us, whether we know it or not, whether we like it or not.

The quality of our lives from now on will depend on science and uses we make of it, for its advance will alter our concepts of life, death, individual identity, and every variety of human relationship.

Are you ready to be "where the action is?" Then consider the first question asked by Robert Schwartz, a senior vice-president at Farley Manning Associates, head of the agency's science department, and public relations counsel to the Upjohn Company.

"What do you read? That's the first question I ask kids interested in this field," Mr. Schwartz said, a former newspaperman with fourteen years executive experience in science public relations, and a member of Phi Beta Kappa.

"That's right, what do you read? Most read little or nothing. No time, they say. I was talking to college youngsters up in Syracuse recently. Maybe they read a newspaper every day. Maybe they glanced at a weekly magazine. But *thinking* magazines—*Harper's, Atlantic,* or books—no time." He shook his head, "Well, that's crazy!"

"The one thing that's essential is an open mind. An open, acquisitive mind. You've got to be aware of everything around you and understand some of the reasons for what's going on. Marketing, for instance. That's part of PR. Today marketing involves many minority groups—the racial situation is a problem. You've got to understand the complexes and problems involved. You must know something about the sociology of minority groups and understand cultural problems."

The phone interrupted. Someone was calling about an insulin molecule—needed a photograph of one. Schwartz told the caller he'd check Upjohn's library to see if any pictures of the human insulin molecule were filed there; he also referred the caller to a University of Pittsburgh scientist who had worked in the area. The caller? An editor of *Science et Vie,* a French magazine.

"We're always getting calls like that," he smiled. "Where were we? Yes—what do you *do* in science PR? Well, you keep in close touch with the press. You must know what kind of material they'll use. You can't write or turn out anything blindly.

"We work with all the media—the drug trade, the professional press. That's scientific and medical journals. And the lay press, of course. Some radio and TV, particularly ET and FM.

"You stay in close touch with the client, naturally. There's a full-time man out at Upjohn doing research for us, getting new material to us."

The actual work itself is only half the picture in science PR, Mr. Schwartz believes. Public relations involves *two* key functions:

1. Analyzing the problem. This requires the following qualities:
—open mind
—curiosity
—creativity
—knowledgeability
—acquisitiveness

2. Solving the problem through communication. This requires:
—ability to write
—ability to listen

The ability to listen means more than just hearing words, although most people don't really hear or listen, Mr.

Schwartz contends. It's the *implication* of what someone says that's so important—to hear beyond what's actually being said.

The academic background for working effectively in science public relations will be discussed in Chapter 15. How do you actually get into the field? Work in a peripheral area, if possible. Get a job on one of the science publications and do any kind of work: proofread, do research, be an errand boy. Read all you can. Or go to work in the public relations department of a university or college. The university press offices turn out a considerable amount of science news. Get a job on a newspaper, but read all the scientific journals you can put your hands on. Get familiar with the language.

The rewards of working in this area of PR? Excellent—if you're good. More important than the money, according to Schwartz, is the sense of satisfaction that comes from dealing with important issues. Remember, "Science Is Where the Action Is."

Financial public relations. Here's another kind of action, another kind of world; this world is equally demanding of PR aspirants who can think, are concerned with economics, and want to know what's going on in the world.

The growth of participation in the investment business in less than fifteen years is remarkable. The number of individual shareholders has spiraled from 6.5 million in 1952 to more than 21 million in 1966. Financial experts predict that within ten years, the number of shareholders will soar to 30 million. The number of outstanding shares of firms listed on the New York Stock Exchange alone has more than doubled during the past decade, to more than 10.2 billion. This number is expected to double again by 1975. The average daily volume of shares traded has increased 400 percent over the past ten years. A staggering total of 8.6 million shares was traded in 1966. This volume will continue to grow, according to predictions.

Shareholders are becoming better informed. As more stock is traded, more individuals become market-minded, and more and more information about the market and the companies is requested.

Where does the information come from? The companies themselves, of course, and more often than not today via the financial public relations man or department.

Financial public relations defined. John F. Moynahan, president of John F. Moynahan, Inc., New York, another of the country's leading PR firms, gives this general definition in the Winter 1966 edition of *Public Relations Quarterly:*

"That area of public relations which relates to the dissemination of information that affects the understanding of stockholders and investors generally concerning the financial position and prospects of a company, and includes among its objectives the improvement of relations between corporations and their stockholders."

A closer look into this business. On the corner of Fifty-fourth and Park Avenue in New York City a huge building soars skyward—the imposing home of First National City Bank, one of the world's largest financial institutions. Inside the ultra-modern lobby there's a special bank of elevators marked "Executives."

A car takes you up on the twenty-ninth floor. A bright corner office with floor to ceiling windows overlooking the upper east side of Manhattan is the hub of this giant bank's public relations activity: it's the office of Ward B. Stevenson, vice-president, public relations, and former president of the Public Relations Society of America.

"The only reason for financial public relations is to enable the financial community to evaluate properly a company's securities," the boyish-looking man said firmly. "Financial publicity is the business of disclosure, as contrasted with promotion. In financial PR, you're not pushing a product."

Stevenson grinned from behind his modern black teak

desk. "Actually, financial PR has pretty well-defined rules to follow. The SEC rules and regulations have the force and effect of law. Anyone working in financial PR must know them, must obey them. And there's no excuse for not knowing them," he added.

The SEC rules are controls established by the Securities & Exchange Commission back in 1933 and 1934 when the Securities Act and the Securities Exchange Act were formulated. Regulations have changed markedly since then— there's a whole new group of legal precedents and rulings. But financial PR is the one defined category of public relations where the law lays definite ground rules which must be followed.

One of the SEC rulings, for example, requires immediate disclosure of any corporate news that could affect stock values. Until recently, many big companies distributed corporate earning news to the wire services or financial press with a request that it be released at a specific time or day. The reason was that many PR men thought that morning or evening papers would give the story more space or prominence, depending on the release "break." However, this did give some people advance knowledge about a particular company and its performance, enabling them to act on the knowledge if they chose to. Today the news must be reported immediately.

"If our Board declares a dividend, the news must be on the news wire *before* the meeting is adjourned, "Stevenson reported.

The reason for SEC intervention and greater regulation is to protect the public—that public of over twenty million investors who own stock today.

The financial community—the target or "public" financial PR people hope to reach, inform and undoubtedly influence —covers a great scope. It includes the institutional investors —foundations, mutual funds, banks, security analysts, and investment advisors, the customer's men in brokerage houses. The business press is one channel or way to reach this public.

Another way that financial PR people arrange to get their company's story told to the right public—say the security analysts—is to set up a presentation.

Security analysts "think" for thousands of investors. The analysts are skilled in the study of a company and its securities, and their recommendations can affect the movement of the stock. Almost all major banks, trust funds, mutual funds, brokerage houses and insurance companies employ analysts to advise on investments. In this way they "think" for the countless people who own shares in mutual funds or whose money is invested for them by banks or insurance companies. Analysts also prepare market letters for brokerage houses, and these in turn influence individual investors.

Your boss may be given an hour to tell the story of where his company is today and where it's going. It's *your* job to see that he has all the ammunition he needs—facts, first of all, well presented. Many financial PR experts think that transparencies do the most effective "telling" job—visuals projected on a screen that tell how the company is organized, portray the management structure, give marketing facts, and outline plans for the future.

When you're a pro in financial PR, you must be able to anticipate questions that analysts might ask your president following his presentation. This means a lot of spadework with your company's comptroller and the president himself. You really must *know* your company or client. These are typical questions you should anticipate:

—Why don't you retire outstanding preferred stock?

—Why did you go to the bond market instead of issuing more stock?

—What are the dilution factors resulting from stock issued in exchange for acquired stock?

These are typical questions, and your president himself might find them hard to answer if he's not prepared to do so. But this will all come when you're a pro; now, where do you begin?

You must know accounting, first of all; economics is a must. You should have a degree—primarily, according to Stevenson, "because you'll be dealing with people who have degrees, many with advanced degrees. You'll be at a disadvantage without one."

Your first job would include all of these tasks: writing a news release on quarterly earnings; taking the release to various people for approval—the comptroller, your company's lawyer, and the chief executive officer. You might work on news leaflets or dividend enclosures. You might help write copy, do research or work with the photo editor on the annual report. You might also handle routine correspondence from stockholders. In short, your work will cover nearly every area of financial public relations activity, to some degree.

Possible pitfalls. Everyone makes mistakes, but in financial PR, two mistakes can be one too many. Transpose one figure on a typewriter and you're in trouble. *Always check the accuracy of figures.* When you're writing a quarterly report, be sure you include comparative figures from the previous year.

Know your company or client. Learn all you can about your company, from every aspect of management to how products are distributed. The more you know, the better equipped you'll be to do a good financial PR job. The financial press will recognize your knowledge—or lack of it—immediately.

"Generally speaking, men and women who report financial news are extremely skilled reporters," financial PR VP Stevenson believes. "The point is, they can't be kidded.

They're ladies and gentlemen who really know their business."

This view is shared by the editorial side of the desk. In an article in the *Public Relations Journal,* Thomas E. Mullaney, business and financial editor of *The New York Times,* says this about business reporters:

"Who is this 'new breed' reporter? He is a skeptical, probing, higher-paid reporter who has earned a master's degree or has had some specialized economic training, who has diversified interests and a broad background, who is more at home assimilating a handful of documents and abhors the superficial press release, who feels a compulsion to get at the heart of an issue, who is not content to deal with any one other than the top authority in the field he is investigating, who is alert, intelligent, skilled and who is an individual of unassailable ethical standards."

If you're interested in the world of financial public relations, there's a great future for you *only* if you're also interested in the elements which make up this world—economics, marketing, management production; everything that contributes to the financial results must be your business.

PR man Stevenson offers this important advice to aspirants: "Keep your mouth shut! When you work in financial public relations, you'll be privy to information shared only by one or two others. Keep it to yourself. Your work is not material for cocktail party conversation. Talk about anything, but *not* your company's business. If you do talk too much, you'll find yourself looking for another job."

What about politics and government PR? Dictionary definitions of the terms "politics," "political" and "government" obviously tend to intertwine—as do public relations activities revolving around government and political figures and situations.

For example, during one three-month period in 1965 Cabinet members held 100 news conferences; the Department of Agriculture alone turned out more than three thousand press releases. President Johnson was attributed with holding more informal press gatherings than any other President in history. The question of what is political and what reflects strictly non-partisan governmental activity is debatable! The facts are that increasingly more efforts are made to "talk" to various publics—to inform, to communicate with and occasionally educate the people to which every government agency or individual is responsible.

Who is doing this "talking"? Every governmental agency, office, division and sub-division, as well as every politician and political hopeful who can gain attention long enough to state a case or push a cause. If this seems exaggerated, consider these facts—and start with the top office in the land, the Presidency. Franklin Roosevelt, in his three-plus terms, held 998 press conferences; Mr. Truman during his tenure as President met with the press formally more than 300 times; General Eisenhower cut this number to approximately 200; and during John F. Kennedy's short time in office, a formal press conference was held about every two weeks.

A formal press conference, according to Richard L. Strout, Washington correspondent for the *Christian Science Monitor,* is when "as many as 300 correspondents may be present and the whole thing is on a more impersonal level."

Mr. Strout, speaking in *Editor & Publisher* (April 2, 1966), continued that "a formal question and answer exchange is a psychologically sound method of presenting complicated government issues in a way the public can understand.

"Alas," Mr. Strout continued, "this tradition has not been continued in recent days. President Johnson has been one of the most accessible men to the press of any President, that is, in informal gatherings, meetings with bureau chiefs, or tips to favorite correspondents. But as for *formal* press conferences, I can only figure that he had *nine* last year. So far in 1966 he has held only *one*."

George Reedy, former White House Press Secretary, was questioned about complaints about the President's methods of conducting press conferences during an address he gave at the Overseas Press Club in New York on June 28. He replied:

"The standpoint of how the President presents himself to the press is up to him. It may or may not be to his own advantage to have conferences on TV, in his office, in a theatre. I have some sympathy with the press but I feel that some reporters want things handed to them. I prefer the newsman who goes in and gets the story. Digging for it is good for the soul."

How much a man is guided by his advisors is his own decision. Calvin Coolidge invented the first "White House spokesman;" Herbert Hoover had no press secretary as such, and only a few press conferences; the first official press secretary was Steve Early, under Franklin Roosevelt—and the famous "Fireside Chats" were innovated; General Eisenhower introduced radio and television into formal press conferences. President Johnson, who inherited one press secretary, Pierre Salinger, has appointed three different men to that post: George Reedy, Bill Moyers and Robert Fleming.

Perhaps one of the most ill-advised developments involving public opinion and the public impression of President Johnson was his post-operative discussion with the press. "Two operations for the price of one" was reviewed in *Life* on October 29, 1965; on October 21, the world's largest daily newspaper, *The Daily News* in New York, had the picture of the President of the United States pointing out his gall bladder incision. The same picture, serviced nation-wide via newswires, appeared everywhere. The negative effect of this gesture is still rankling in some quarters of the country!

The problem of *good* public relations is a vital one, from the top office right down the line.

Pierre Salinger told the PRSA delegates attending their annual meeting in Denver (August, 1965) that "the entire public relations of the White House is handled by seven people—three men and four women. That has been the size of the staff in the White House press office since Steve Early took over for FDR in 1932." He went on to say that "the Defense and State departments have literally hundreds in this field."

Nearly every department of the government has an information director, press officer or public relations representative—although the term "PR" man is seldom acknowledged. The Army, Navy, Air Force, Peace Corps, NASA, USIA— each has its own bureau or department for public relations activity. Here's an example of activity involved, quoted from the March 21 issue of *PR Reporter:*

"In its crash campaign to inform the nation's 19 million Medicare eligibles that they must register by March 31, the government has spread the word through Social Security and welfare agencies and sent reams of publicity used over and over again by newspapers and radio/TV.

"Anyone who doesn't know the facts by now must be pretty inaccessible. *Yet another $7 million* was appropriated about two weeks ago to hire several thousand people around the country who will call on newspapers and radio/TV just to make *sure* they're using the publicity releases."

Another report on another aspect of governmental activity comes from Warren Rogers' column in the December 7, 1965, New York *Journal American:* "The Astronauts and Their Wives." Writing from the Manned Space Center in Houston, Rogers said:

"It is astonishing how hard they work here to maintain the All-American Boy image of America's astronauts. . . . It stands to reason that the astronauts are flesh and blood with individual characteristics, good and bad, just like all the rest of us. But all you get from the earnest news-managers here —and I'm told that there are no less than 64 employed at the Center to deal with the press—is an unmarked image of all the astronauts as trustworthy, loyal, kind, brave, clean and reverent. . . . Perhaps, in time the National Aeronautics and Space Administration [NASA] will ease up on its brain-washing."

NASA has its troubles—far beyond the image of the astronauts. In the May 30, 1966, issue of *The New York Times*, NASA Chief James Webb declared on a page 1 story:

"The nation is facing a crisis in space planning . . . The question is what to do with the vast, $20-billion Apollo project after men have landed on the moon."

The article continued, "Mr. Webb, a vigorous and voluble man, has been trying to tell Congress and the public about Apollo's present and future problems for many months. He is disappointed and even dismayed that neither audience seems to have got the message."

Carrying this concern to a specific public, the men who read *Space/Aeronautics* magazine, editorial writer John Campbell says:

"Selling the American people on getting to the moon first was not too difficult. Selling the country on what it needs to maintain its new leadership will be a vastly harder job. Yet if we fail, we may find that we have won a dubious race to the moon only to lose the 20th Century."

These various examples of public relations activities of different government areas and agencies, each with a different responsibility to the public or special publics, are random items illustrating *one consistent pattern: poor public relations*. Similar examples and situations can be found in every newspaper and magazine, on newscasts and radio program. Poor public relations, stemming from a government activity, a misguided mayor's action ("Mayor's 'Free' Car to

Run Up City Bills," *World Telegram and Sun*, January 28, 1966), to ill-directed funds in the village clerk's office, have powerful and often long-lasting consequences.

PR specialists in areas of government and politics are far too few; yet this is an area where the sound, knowledgeable public relations person could be infinitely valuable. The general job category for this kind of public relations work is a non-profit association classification. When you work with an individual politican, your role might be that of press agent —depending on the man's stature. Regardless, the dynamics of sound public relations are demanded for effective results, and there's too little of it today.

John Hill, the dean of public relations, on receiving the American Academy of Achievement Golden Plate award in Dallas declared:

"The role of public relations in the opinion-forming process is to communicate information and viewpoint on behalf of causes and organizations. The objective is to inform the public and win its favor . . . PR people need to examine their tools, their techniques, and procedures in the field of communication and advances of sociology, psychology, and the other sciences."

What about you? Does the realm of government work and politics intrigue you? There's a vital job to be done; in our society, government offices and agencies are increasing in size, authority and number. The need for effective communication and sound public relations also is growing.

In just another decade, when the "Specialists Speak Out," perhaps your work, with one of the top non-profit associations in the land, will be sufficiently effective and meaningful that you will be able to stand up, speak out and be counted.

The world is ready!

12 Public Relations—
Exciting World for Women

"Madison Avenue, U.S.A."—the street where dreams become reality or explode in a cloud of expensive smoke! Madison Avenue is most often associated with the world of advertising, but it's also the home of a few public relations agencies. One is Farley Manning Associates, the antithesis of all that Madison Avenue generally connotes.

High above the busy street, this major PR agency—one of the top ten in the country, according to *Editor & Publisher* —commands most of the floor at 342 Madison Avenue. Open the glistening white New England doors and you step into a small reception room that looks more like a fine old-fashioned parlor—oriental rug, period furniture, a handsome oil painting of a sailing ship on one wall.

The receptionist announces your arrival and a secretary ushers you into the inner sanctum—the elegant, chandelier-lighted office of one of the most successful public relations women in the country, Martha Olson. A tall, attractive brunette, Miss Olson speaks softly with just a touch of her Southern origin still rounding the edges of her speech. She too is the antithesis of a Madison Avenue career woman, for she's quiet, warm and reserved—yet the only woman officer of her company, a vice-president and member of the executive committee.

"What qualities are most desired for PR?" she repeated, swinging her chair. "Well, good judgment is high on the list, I believe. And the ability to listen and analyze problems is important. It helps to be able to communicate," she added with a smile.

What about the future for women? Excellent, she predicts. "There's equal opportunity in all areas." This is one PR executive who doesn't consider specialization a vital factor for success in public relations.

"The basic qualities that make anyone a good general practitioner also make a good specialist. Good judgment, as I said, is very important. You must understand concepts, you must understand abstract ideas. The procedures or techniques for any one special area may differ from another area, but these can be learned. The thinking that makes anyone a good generalist—a sound *general* PR person comes first. Then specialization can follow."

How long does it take for a woman to "make it" in this business? This woman is in her thirties and she's only one of the many women who are making it in public relations. Mark these growth figures: In 1950, the U.S. Bureau of Census listed 2,000 women in public relations and publicity; ten years later that number had jumped to 7,271—a more than 263 *percent* increase in a decade! During the same period, the increase of men in the business was only 40 percent.

The July, 1966, issue of the *Public Relations Journal* reported a survey on women in PR which indicates the girls are really on the go. Among the women surveyed, 360 members of PRSA (the leading professional association of public relations executives), the average salary was $11,358. Two-thirds of the women earned between $6,000 and $13,000 annually, and 11 percent earned more than $20,000. The top salary reported in this survey was $40,000. (Incidentally, these figures are *less* than men make in comparable jobs, according to similar surveys. This situation is improving, but it's still a fact of life, girls!)

According to results from this survey among women in PR, successful women in public relations work in the same areas as men—they're not limited to "strictly female" areas. In fact, nearly two-thirds of the respondents either owned or were partners in their own firms and cited a client roster of considerable range: financial corporations, heavy industries, unions, local, state and federal agencies, politicians, oil drillers, breweries, to name a few. Only about one-third of this group reported their activities were concentrated in "women's work" areas.

The importance of *women's interest* areas in public relations is important to girls considering the field, however, for several reasons. Women's interest covers a lot of territory, first of all. Nearly every consumer product made and sold has some direct or indirect appeal to women. It's a matter of simple economics. Women do the buying today. If precedence is any pattern maker, women will do more buying tomorrow— of everything from automobiles and real estate to a sink stopper for that pesky drain! More than 80 percent of all purchases in this country are made by women; the ladies not only are wearing the pants, they're also buying them! Even 87 percent of men's furnishings are selected by women. More than half of the total shares of stock in American business are held by women.

Nearly every product and every public relations problem has its own particular women's interest aspect. There are, indeed, certain areas where a woman's touch or thinking is preferable. In fashion, food, home furnishings—the obvious distaff categories—girls will find many fascinating jobs in PR; these can serve as a springboard to more general work in public relations or can prove a testing ground for specialization within the framework of "women's work."

The fashion industry. Public relations jobs in the nation's fourth largest industry—a multi-billion dollar one—can range from working in a small shop where everyone does everything—interviewing the governor's wife and putting stamps on the envelope containing the story—to directing the activities of a fifteen-girl staff in a major fiber company.

Working in fashion PR presumes an interest and some knowledge of the field. It helps to have good taste, too—that amorphous quality that will decide whether you're a real pro or just another publicist working in fashion. All the basics which have been discussed—an ability to write, learning how to work with the various media, knowing the requirements of a particular paper, radio station or magazine— apply to fashion, of course. There's a language in fashion that's almost unique. Where else is a bracelet fun, or a long torso line important? In fashion, hair swings, bosoms ride high, skirts skim over knees and coats stand away from the body! *Happenings* began in fashion—way back in 1902, *Harper's Bazaar* reported a "Paris Happening" for the first time!

The terminology is a must to know, use with restraint, and *not* abuse. Learn all you can by reading the magazines, the groovy ones! Read the others, too—*Atlantic, Harper's, The Reporter*—know what's going on everywhere. *Want* to know what's going on. The dullest girl in the world is the fashion publicist who looks and talks as though she stepped from a page in a fashion magazine. Chances are she's a poor PR person, too, because everything's on the surface.

Where are the publicity jobs in fashion? In a large city, primarily, although every good-sized department store has a publicity department—whether it's one overworked woman or a staff of bright young things. J. L. Hudson's, for example, has an excellent public relations operation—constantly creating, coordinating and promoting events to focus attention on this retail empire in Detroit.

Retail stores offer one kind of opportunity in fashion; another is with the fiber producers, who all have active public relations. The Cotton Council's Maid of Cotton PR project brings a pretty Southern girl into leading department stores each year, sporting a complete cotton wardrobe created by America's top designers. You can buy it, right in your local store! The Wool Bureau, du Pont, Celanese, Dow Chemical, Chemstrand have staffs of skilled, trained people working hard in public relations to tell various publics about their particular product.

The pattern companies are another category for fashion-oriented public relations activity. Singer Sewing sponsors its Singer Sew-Off each year, giving thousands of dollars in prizes to clever young seamstresses; Simplicity Patterns, Advance Patterns, Coats and Clark—all have busy PR campaigns directed to specific groups, to interest and influence these groups with their particular fashion message.

Seventh Avenue, New York City, the hub of the nation's garment industry, offers varied opportunities in public relations and publicity for fashion-minded girls. Most manufacturers have publicity women or work with public relations agencies. Various associations within the fashion industry have public relations programs. The Millinery Institute, the Leather Institute, FIFC (Fur Information Fashion Council) —almost every fashion-oriented association has a team of public relations experts expounding their message to a given audience. (Association members are several manufacturers in the same business—as furriers, shoe companies, etc.)

An editor speaks about fashion publicists. Eugenia Sheppard, the petite dean of New York City's newspaper fashion editors (Women's Editor of the *Herald Tribune* for years and women's editor of the *World Journal Tribune* in New York), says flatly, "Few fashion publicists do a good job."

This demure, Dresden-like editor, famous for her peppery personality, controls one of the mightiest women's pages in the country. Countless publicists, both in New York and from fashion headquarters elsewhere, hope to work with this influential editor. More could, if they knew their business better!

"They just don't care how they write, most of them. I prefer facts only. Give me an idea. If it's good, I'll assign someone to follow up. Instead, publicists send me a list of their accounts.

"How often someone has called me and said, 'I thought you might be interested in our new account.' I couldn't care less!" Books, papers and copy towered on the two huge desks in Miss Sheppard's office, nearly dwarfing the tiny blonde dynamo seated next to the typewriter at one desk. "Never mind what *you* think," she continued. "Is it a good story? Journalism training is important, I think. It helps organize thoughts."

The qualities Miss Sheppard believes are important for a fashion publicist include integrity, understanding, knowledge of your job, and knowing what the editor can use. She also mentioned sophistication. This quality may be a gift of time!

Women's work—another voice and view. Publicity and PR girls, no matter what their women's interest area may be, usually work with syndicate editors. Helen Hennessy, women's editor of one of the country's largest syndicates, NEA, a nationally syndicated news feature service, was equally outspoken about PR people.

"Know what you're talking about! Most of you don't know enough about the product or company."

Miss Hennessy is a warm, attractive woman who resembles actress Shelley Winters. "If you don't know the answer, say you don't. Find out, but don't try and bluff your way through!

"One thing about fashion publicists," Miss Hennessy continued, "too often they adopt the same aura as a fashion magazine editor. It's fine for magazine girls. But the fashion publicist loses sight of what her job is; she uses jargon that's too 'in.' She forgets that most of the world interested in fashion speaks plain English!"

Work in fashion PR. Your actual job in fashion publicity and public relations will vary with the area, kind of company, the scope of the operation, and other factors. Generally, fashion PR includes publicizing each collection or line, editorial photography (often on location or away from a studio), working with all the media, covering the fabric market, keeping up with all fashion news, writing copy, helping with press shows—everything from preparing a news story to zipping a model into her dress during a fashion show. Some of your work will be exciting, much will be downright drudgery: stuffing envelopes, stapling, pasting up reports on boards and running errands.

The publicity director of *Seventeen* magazine, Jean Baer, says that "fashion publicity is really hard physical work!" This dark-haired, bubbly young woman said she looks for assistants who don't mind the prospect of working hard.

"One time a helper in our department put on some white gloves before we began collating a mailing—she didn't want to ruin her nails. I knew she'd never make it in publicity!" The girl moved to the editorial side of the magazine, Miss Baer commented, and did well.

"A good publicist must be able to do more than one thing simultaneously. She's the kind of person who can talk on the phone and file her nails at the same time. But I mean at home," she added quickly.

Food—plain and fancy. Another area where a girl's talents are particularly important is in the food industry—another billion-dollar giant, and growing. The public relations departments of the big food companies offer many opportunities, ranging from food preparation, testing, photography, promotion, to going out and working with the media—perhaps directly on camera.

Phyllis Berlowe, a food specialist with Edward Gottlieb Associates, handles public relations and publicity for the Thomas J. Lipton Company.

"Food publicity work is fascinating, and different from other publicity," Miss Berlowe believes. "It's directed to the homemaker, who's bombarded with ideas on how to feed her family. And we service editors must show a homemaker what's new, what's economical as well as nutritious. We must know how to write recipes, too. That's a special kind of writing. It must be brief, exact, yet cover all aspects."

Preparing food for photography is a specialty, too, Miss Berlowe explained. "Food must look appetizing and not appear too professionally prepared, because then the average homemaker won't try it. Some food isn't very photogenic," Miss Berlowe grinned. "Spinach or beets look disgusting—absolutely black."

Food PR people work with all the media; newspaper food and syndicate editors want completed features with pretested recipes. Magazines are divided into two categories. One is the major consumer publications, which have their own test kitchens. Food people give them ideas, and when they're accepted, the editors usually develop the ideas into a story or article. The other classification is the smaller magazines—romance publications, the professional magazines for home economists. These smaller publications, which reach an important public, often will work closely with PR departments of food companies or their public relations agencies to have special material created just for them.

One quality a girl should have to work successfully as a food specialist in PR, according to Miss Berlowe, is a basic interest in food. Miss Berlowe, a trim young woman with a figure which belies her test kitchen work, also believes that you must know about nutrition, be interested in economics, and have a genuine desire to help families know more about good nutrition.

At home in PR. Still another major category for women's-interest public relations activity is the expanding home furnishings field. Many of the big furniture manufacturers have their own PR departments, or the work is handled in an agency. The big fiber companies have girls who work only in the home furnishings area, to create greater awareness of fibers for the home—used in draperies, rugs, furniture coverings, even on walls!

PR work in home furnishings requires basic knowledge of the industry. You must know something about furniture, how it's made and its care; you should know decorating, its important periods and influences. You learn how to "set up" a room for photography—create a real-looking room or corner that will photograph and reproduce well. You'll probably go to the big furniture market shows in Chicago and High Point, South Carolina. You'll learn to set a handsome table, a smart buffet, or design a baby's room. Your work probably will include writing booklets, creating publicity material, travel and demonstrations before groups and occasionally in department stores.

Your newspaper publicity will be directed to the women's page editors, so "know what you're talking about"; base your statements on available facts. This is one area where research is relatively easy and essential for effective PR activity.

"She walks in beauty." With apologies to Lord Byron, she'd better forget the poetry and dig out facts, if she's working in cosmetics PR!

The business of beauty is a serious one and a highly profitable area for publicity and PR work. The biggest advertisers in magazines like *Vogue* and *Harper's Bazaar* are cosmetics companies, and their sales are growing. As madame (and now monsieur) becomes increasingly concerned with ways to be more beguiling, she'll spend money for the means. Fortunately, or unfortunately, our society is possessed by a youth complex; to look young, if not *be* young, is an obsession with most Americans today, and cosmetics companies are crowding to board this profitable merry-go-round.

There is a valid publicity job to be done for cosmetics. New products must be introduced, claims must be examined and presented honestly, beauty photography is a special skill. There are two common pitfalls in cosmetics publicity:

—*Exaggeration.* "Turn back the years, smooth away wrinkles, look young in a month." Honestly! What are the *facts* about the product? What does it *claim* to do; where and when can a reader get it?

—*Poor planning.* The amount of second-rate cosmetics publicity material that crosses an editor's desk is astonishing. Pictures with too much product emphasis; words-words-words spilling over the page, saying nothing. Too frequent releases, nothing new, and little or no awareness of what an editor wants to know.

Joan Kaiser, the fashion and beauty editor of one of this country's largest papers, the Los Angeles *Herald Examiner*, thinks that beauty publicity particularly is a misguided and wasteful effort.

"It's dull! Worse than that, it's inaccurate. Many major papers have research departments. Facts *must* be accurate. You'd be surprised at the claims some of the products make," she scowled. "Why, one man tried to tell me his product got rid of varicose veins when it was applied. When I challenged him, it turned out he was talking about superficial skin veins. I was furious!"

This pretty editor has made it her business to learn as much as possible about the beauty business. She's not alone. Editors are a knowledgeable lot, and your own knowledge must be deeper than just surface if you want to be a really successful beauty PR pro.

Miss Kaiser confirms that few firms or agencies bother to learn enough about the media they want to work with. To find out exactly what information a woman's page editor wants about a product, fashion or idea, she suggests an inquiry be directed to the editor. Outline questions on a postcard. Most editors will return it answered, and you'll know the exact requirements of a particular paper. This means work for you, lots of it. But it also means you'll get more and better publicity for your client or company. Ask the editor her requirements regarding:

—retail outlets (does she need them?)
—a fact sheet (does she want it?)
—use of color photography (color chromes or R.O.P. mats
—specially produced mats or matrix for color reproduction in newspapers)
—product pictures: with or without a model
—deadlines for special sections

Woman's world. The prospects for women in public relations go well beyond the confines of distaff interests. The areas of fashion, homemaking, beauty and cosmetics are vital to our economy, and woman's aptitudes often are highly desirable for many of the jobs in these huge industries. These areas are springboards for specialization within the respective fields, or they may prove an entree into new and different territories.

One woman who claims her job in public relations is now involved with "dogs, daughters and delphiniums" is Mrs. Elizabeth Carpenter, Press Secretary and Staff Director for Mrs. Lyndon B. Johnson.

Mrs. Carpenter, a vital, outgoing woman with a biting wit, spoke to the PRSA New York chapter at a luncheon meeting in March, 1966. The Empire Room of the Waldorf-Astoria was jammed with public relations executives who wanted to hear Mrs. Carpenter. The talk was scheduled shortly after a famous French chef had left the White House, and Mrs. Carpenter commented, "René could cook chili, all right. It was just the flaming brandy he poured over it!" The bi-partisan audience loved it!

Her message, to an audience whose business is communications, focused on Mrs. Johnson's beautification program. Each luncheon place had a copy of "Ideas for beauty-minded people," an attractive brochure dedicated "To you, who love this great nation . . ."

The brochure, a tasteful and tactful compilation of "Make America Beautiful" ideas, was directed to various facets of society: civic and service organizations, businessmen, manufacturers, the press, home owners, even the school child. Most of the guests took it home, so someone else saw it!

Her speech was equally effective for this particular audience or public: she discussed the Great Society's three goals —beautification, cultural growth, and war on poverty, all in terms of "you." What can *you* do about reaching these goals? "Influence your companies to be receptive to the ideas," she suggested. "Make personnel directors aware of the underprivileged in your communities. The Great Society must be created across the land—not just in Washington."

Mrs. Carpenter made the audience feel the job belonged to each one individually. It's *your* responsibility.

A PR technique? Of course. An effective one? Absolutely. Each man and woman listening to Liz Carpenter at that luncheon felt strong stirrings to do more for his country. Some, perhaps, acted on the impulse.

More and more, women are moving into responsible roles and positions. Public relations is a job of and with authority. Columnist Sylvia Porter wrote on June 14, 1966, in the New York *Post*, "There is no alternative to an ever rising use of intelligent and competent woman-power." By 1970, there will be twenty-eight million women working. If you're interested in public relations, there's an exciting and rewarding future ahead for you. The responsibility of earning success is *yours*.

As the oval mirror said to the girl examining her reflection, "Here's looking at you!"

13 Pick a Day—
Any Day

Carpe diem. It's your day to savor a full nine-to-five sojourn in a bona-fide public relations job—in an agency, a big company, or an association. What goes on behind the glittering glass facade of a Manhattan PR office door? What really happens when you hang a hat on a worn hook in the public relations department of a steel company? What do you do in that cozy cubicle assigned to the public relations director's assistant in downtown Meadville's Mental Health Association office?

Try it for a day.

Hurry with the crowd along New York City's streets churning with early morning traffic; edge—or push—your way up the subway exit, speed along the sidewalk, dash with countless others into one of the yawning arched entrances of a midtown skyscraper. Turn into your bank of elevators, tap the button for your floor, ignore the piped music meant to brighten your morning, move smartly through the heavy glass doors of Public Relations-International, your company. Smile at the receptionist as you glance at the clock above her head—8:47 A.M. Just made it! Hurry down the carpeted corridor to one of the small, glass-enclosed offices lining one side of the hall—*your* office for the past few months. You're a full-fledged PR junior now. Another agency day is about to begin.

The first thing you do after settling down at your desk is review the daily checklist you made up last night, just before leaving. It noted yesterday's activities for your work report and reminded you of items left to do. You've learned to be more orderly—it makes your work simpler.

Three calls to make—the photographer for the location job; a follow-up call to your clipping bureau, because they're still sending duplicates of the syndicate story; and a confirmation of a booking with a model agency. This can all be done this morning; next you check your daily calendar. A major client is coming in, and your boss had mentioned you might be asked to sit in on part of the morning session. You hope he remembers!

Mail is delivered. The office boy drops your small stack noisily into your "In" box with a hurried "Hi." Next year a secretary might open it for you—now it's one of your jobs! Clippings for one client, carbons of letters routed within your company regarding one of your accounts, promotional material from an airline, two trade papers, a memo from your vice-president suggesting everyone arrive by 9 A.M., and a request for additional tear sheets of a business story on one of your clients that appeared in the *Wall Street Journal.* You read the mail, thumb through the trade papers and put one aside to take home for further reading, call your mailroom to order reprints of the business story, and as you finish the memo requesting punctuality, your account supervisor stops to remind you of the client meeting—"Bring your coffee along."

The meeting gets underway quickly. Executive VP, director of marketing, public relations director, advertising agency account executive, and six marketing committee members of the client company sit around the table in your conference room. The client, a Chicago-based association of furniture manufacturers, with member companies throughout the United States, Canada and various international affiliates, is meeting to review a name change and identification. You had read all the material available, of course, and your job this morning would be to listen, observe and take notes.

"All right, gentlemen, let's see the logo, first of all." At this signal, the advertising account exec opens a briefcase filled with a dozen large cardboard sheets covered with brilliant blue paper. Each contains a handsomely designed symbol for the association; most of the artwork utilizes the familiar golden shield the organization had used for years for member companies and advertising. Other samples depart completely—one suggests a modern four-poster bed, which the executive vice-president thought might suggest sleeping on the job. Everyone chuckles—though it isn't particularly amusing to you.

As the symbol choice is reviewed, discussion covers advisability of changing the organization's name to emphasize the international aspects of the business, and the ramifications of name change—from member notification to a complete publicity program to explain the change to the business community and consumers. You listen closely, because you might be assigned to work on the consumer aspects of the program. You'd better know why the symbol is being revised, why the name is changing, and anything else you can learn about the client during this meeting. The strongest dissenter to any change is a man from Europe—a director of the organization's chapter in Rome. His objection focuses on a loss of international identity in a new logo and name, since the Europeans are even more familiar than Americans with the old symbol. You make a note to discuss with your boss the advisability of preparing a special education program for foreign members of the organization. You also discover this kind of meeting involves a considerable amount of extraneous conversation—and before you realize it, it is noon.

The officers of the client organization, the ad man, and your boss all leave for a special luncheon at the Four Seasons. Whenever this particular client comes into the city, one special lunch is arranged, and maybe one day you'll be invited. Not this day, however!

Back to your desk; check phone calls—several messages waiting for you, two of them repeat calls from yesterday. You check your watch—12:20; better order a sandwich and organize the rest of your day.

Your afternoon begins shortly after 1 P.M.; confirm your photography date, check with the model agency—everything is okay. Write a news release on a new product—your drug company client has a new cleanser for "troubled teen skin." You'd better double-check all the facts on this one. Maybe some special research is in order. A second mail brings in more clips. One editor in Indiana used a story of yours verbatim; must write her. And sometime today, you'd better review your morning meeting notes and type them into a report for your boss.

Five-fifteen in the afternoon. Where did the day go?

You still haven't accomplished all you had hoped to do, and tonight you'll have to read up on the skin cleanser research data. Tomorrow you'll be out on location with the shooting assignment for at least a couple of hours.

Agency life? Great! Now out to battle the world hurrying home. The frantic pace is part of the endless challenge in the city—*your* city!

Another day dawns—this one in the friendly warmth of a Midwestern city. You ride in a car pool to work, your destination: the public relations department of a medium-sized steel mill sprawled on the outskirts of town. Your job? PR assistant.

You've already put in a couple of weeks on the job; the first day or two you spent meeting people in your own department and other people you'll be working with—men and women in personnel, sales and advertising. Your boss arranged for you to tour the mill—an exciting, noisy, confusing junket through huge cavern-like buildings manned by brawny, busy steelmakers wearing goggles and heavy gloves. On this first trip, you probably couldn't tell a rolling mill from a blast furnace, but as you become more familiar with your job, you'll soon know how steel is made, who makes it, where it goes, what your big customers use it for, how it's shipped, priced, and packed. Every facet of the business will be your business.

As part of your indoctrination, your boss gave you a stack of booklets to read, and at first this material was confusing, but it soon became clear and helpful to you. Very often, indoctrination material for a beginner in PR will include a corporate history, an organization chart, recent annual reports and back issues of the company newspaper or magazine.

Tours and type are only an introduction, however. You really get to know your company through talks with fellow employees, keen observation of what goes on around you, research you'll do for specific assignments.

Now you've been working a week or two, and your day gets under way. You'll probably start work at 8:30 or 9 in the morning and you'll have one or two continuing assignments. One may be to help out on the house organ (a term used to describe a company publication). The publication at your steel mill is an internal one which means it goes to "insiders" —employees and retired employees. It's a twelve-page magazine published monthly and mailed to the employees' homes so that the families can read it. The editor is responsible for planning, writing, layout and production; you're assigned to him as an assistant, so each month you have specific stories to cover.

This month, you're doing a feature story on the safety department and at 10 this morning you have a date to interview the safety director in his office in the Personnel Building. So, first thing you review the material you have on this department and get your questions for the interview clearly in mind. You'll want to ask about safety equipment—"hard hats," goggles, gloves, safety shoes, shields. You'll ask the director about his background and history with the company; get latest reports on the safety awards which have been won by various departments and ask about any new innovations in plant and equipment which have been made to protect the workers. Other questions will come to you as you conduct the interview, but you must have the key areas in mind before you start.

At 10 o'clock sharp you show up at the Personnel Building. The safety director is a wise, experienced man who gives you a great story—answers questions clearly and explains things you don't understand. At the close of the interview, you get some good safety photos from him and make a date with him for the plant photographer to shoot special pictures for your story. The date is tentatively set for the next afternoon—you've got a deadline to meet. But you have to clear it with your photographer, then confirm it with the safety director. It's 11:30 by the time you get back to your office. There, your boss tells you that you'd better plan to go to a special luncheon meeting that day—the president of the company is speaking to the Chamber of Commerce. The editor had been assigned but something hot came up for him to cover instead. Your job: cover the speech for the company newspaper.

You're off to a downtown hotel. The luncheon lasts until two but you've got a good story. The president made some important statements about the company's efforts to control air pollution through multi-million-dollar investments in new stacks and fly-ash control systems. This is good community relations, and it's a development which will interest employees who live in the area. You make a mental note to check the daily newspaper story and then hunt for new angles for your own story. Yours is a monthly, so you can get additional facts the local paper won't have.

It's about 2:30 when you get back to the office; first, you follow through on arrangements for tomorrow's photography. Tell the photographer the type of shots you want, how many, and where to meet you. Then get back to the safety director and confirm the date. Next, your boss gives you the background material on a salesman who has just been promoted to a managerial role in sales. You're to do a short news story for all the trade publications on this personnel change. Again there's a deadline, so while you review the material, you ask the secretary to start typing envelopes to the trade press. When your story is written and approved, it will be ready to mail.

Now it's 3:30—still time to work on the salesman's promotion release. Short, only three or four paragraphs, it's a tight, straightforward news story. It's finished by 4:15, so you take it to your boss for clearance. He reads it, calls the sales office to doublecheck one fact (turns out you're right) and he approves it. Great! You still have time to brief the secretary on the mailing—number of copies to run off, when and how to mail it (first class, air mail), how many prints of the photograph to order, correct caption of the picture, and file copies.

Five o'clock. The day shift has gone home and the tempo in the offices is slowing down. Time to quit. Just to be sure your notes on the safety feature are in order, you take all the material home to review before tomorrow morning. After all, tomorrow will be like today—varied assignments, deadline to meet, people to see, unexpected developments—all part of your daily corporate or company PR job. It's a good life!

Still *another* sunrise—this one welcomes the day in a cheery, well-known Southern city. Although you're not a native, in the few weeks you've been assistant to the PR director of the local Mental Health Association, your speech already reflects the softened corners of a genuine Southern accent!

In this non-profit association job—much like any association or government agency job in the apprentice stage—you've already learned the basic policies of your association as well as the responsibilities of your own job.

In this job you're the "number two" man in a two-man department, since it's unlikely that this type of association would have a big staff. So you two and a part-time secretary carry out all the public relations assignments, reporting to the executive director, the only other paid professional in the organization. A little before 9 in the morning, you arrive at work and look at the jobs already facing you.

There's the paste-up on the monthly newsletter which goes to all past contributors to the association, to editors, and special groups interested in your organization's work. Your association represents both lay people and professionals in the mental health field; therefore the publication must appeal to both. The paste-up shows all type, art, and photos properly positioned.

You'll pick up notes of two or three phone calls which came in yesterday after you left. Your boss, the public information director, says he wants a word with you while you're both having coffee. The phone calls aren't urgent—one is from a printer. "He probably wants to know when he'll get the paste-up," you decide; another is from the chairman of your Speaker's Bureau. "I'll call him later in the morning."

Now, what does the boss have on his mind? Over your first office coffee of the day, he explains that it's time to start planning for the annual fund-raising drive. The campaign is eight months away but successful fund-raising is basic to the very survival of the association; that means you must map your strategy early, start all the groundwork almost as soon as the last check is in from the previous drive!

The public relations director tells you that he wants a checklist of ideas for the new campaign from you. This will give you a great chance to suggest some techniques you've considered and they might give him some fresh approaches to an annual problem. It's agreed you'll review last year's campaign—dates, goals, structure, themes, and costs of various printed material. When you've gone over all of this, you'll put down your ideas with suggested deadlines, themes and formats. At this point, you're not to worry about cost estimates; the boss wants ideas . . . pretend that money is no problem! Put down every conceivable idea for the drive. Also, you don't have to worry about the presentation of your plan—just type it up rough so you can go over it together.

Brain-storming on this has taken an hour—it's almost 10. You must get the newsletter paste-up back to the printer—that's your first job. You've already proofread the type in galley form; now it's a question of one last, careful look at each page to see if any mistakes have slipped in—captions under the wrong pictures, type left out, artwork too dark or photos which overbalance the heads. One hour's work and you're sure that everything now is correct; you initial it and say a silent prayer you haven't overlooked anything. Then you show it to your boss. He glances at it hastily and says "Okay." You call the printer and ask a messenger to pick it up this afternoon.

Now, you call your chairman of the Speaker's Bureau. He's a valuable member of the association's executive committee, a young, dynamic businessman who spends days each month on intensive work for the association. The Speaker's Bureau is your responsibility (except on high-level policy matters) and the chairman wants to meet with you this afternoon to discuss some problems. Fine. The appointment is made for 2 P.M. here at headquarters.

Next, the boss turns over a stack of material on a researcher at an Eastern university who has been doing interesting work on one phase of mental illness. The good news is that this pioneer has agreed to speak at an upcoming meeting of your group. Could you review the technical paper, biographical material and plans for the meeting, then start work on an announcement story for the local newspapers? You'll have to request a glossy photograph of the man—the university forgot to enclose one.

It's now almost 1 P.M.; just time to dash out for a quick sandwich and return in time to review the Speaker's Bureau material before your 2 o'clock meeting. After all, an active Speaker's Bureau is one of the most effective tools you have for reaching key groups in the community with the facts about mental illness—what's being done, what should be done, how each citizen can help.

Your chairman arrives a little late—about 2:30. You talk until 4. The major problem you discuss is the apparent apathy of women's clubs as compared with the active interest shown by men's clubs and professional groups. The Bureau has more requests than it can fill from men's organizations, but requests from women's groups have been declining for the past three months. It's a crucial, complex problem. You promise to consult your boss and find out reasons for this trend, but you also recommend a new letter and brochure which would have more appeal to women. The chairman approves the idea and you promise to get cost estmates on printing and mailing.

By now, you're pretty weary, but you start reading the research paper prepared by the professor. It's fascinating but technical, and rather heavy going. It's 5 P.M. Officially, the day is over; you straighten up your desk and take the research material home with you. It will make tomorrow's work lighter if you have this finished. Another day, several more dollars—and a good feeling of some accomplishment.

The training or first-round jobs in any area of public relations activity are somewhat similar, and you must begin by learning the basics. As you mature in the job, your knowledge and abilities also increase and you start the climb up that long, often fascinating road to success. Are you for public relations? Is PR for you? Check your rating and potential in the next chapter.

14 How Do You Measure Up?

Now you've read the book. You know what the "story" is about, what develops along the way and where the various situations take place. Are you ready for the *action*—the activity that goes into public relations work? Do you have the qualities that are demanded from the pros?

The top public relations practitioners all have clear ideas on the qualities they consider essential for success in the business. Edward L. Bernays, named by *Time* as "U.S. Publicist No. One," declares that of all the personal qualifications, "Character, integrity, and a logical objectivity in the individual practitioner are the really essential attributes of any public relations man worthy of the name."

In his book *The Making of a Public Relations Man,* John Hill says, "Public relations calls for a variety of special experiences, abilities and qualifications. In my opinion the most important single element is integrity, which is a matter of character. Next to integrity I would rank judgment."

A third leading public relations man, Edward Gottlieb, board chairman of the international public relations firm Edward Gottlieb & Associates, offers equally specific views.

"The first and most important quality for a good public relations person is curiosity. Next, I believe a good, broad general education is important. Following that, I consider awareness and sensitivity are significant qualities for public relations.

"Then communication is essential. The ability to communicate clearly and succinctly—the effective communication of ideas, concepts and facts."

Mr. Gottlieb, a former newspaperman who founded his firm nearly twenty years ago, has built his business from a small beginning into one of the leading public relations operations in the United States, with offices throughout the world. Beyond the expected qualities in a successful PR expert, this man has added another dimension: several years ago he survived a major airline crash but was told he would never walk again. Today, Edward Gottlieb walks into his office each morning shortly after 9, without the aid of canes or crutches. He directs a staff of sixty in New York and supervises his offices in major cities throughout the country and world. In addition to the qualities necessary for success in public relations, this man has proved the importance of determination, stamina and courage—essential for success in living. He was asked about "integrity" as a desired quality for PR work.

"Integrity? Why, I take that for granted! Maybe I shouldn't," he added with a twinkling grin, "but I do."

The *Quarterly Review of Public Relations* cited a list of ten qualities considered desirable for anyone interested in PR. How many of these do you have?

1. *Initiative.* Do you take the first step in a new project? Are you willing to undertake the responsibility for originating activity? Do you start things without being told to do so —be honest, now! When the social science teacher asked for a volunteer for a symposium, did you raise your hand? Why not?

2. *Persistence.* "The act of enduring continuance" is a rare quality not to be confused with stubbornness. The latter is a refusal to yield, even when good judgment advises it. Persistence, on the other hand, involves resoluteness and endurance *with an open mind* to accomplish a desired goal.

One of the young men selected for the All-America football team a few years ago, a fullback who was determined to develop his strength to the utmost, followed this self-imposed training schedule: during training and in season, he ran a full-mile course in his home town, strapped down with fifty-pound weights. The result? His perseverance developed this boy into a formidable stone wall—the best fullback on the All-America line. He reached his goal by working persistently toward it. In business, the same dogged determination is important for success.

3. *Drive; ambition.* How much do you have? Some years ago a band director asked his mediocre oboist, "Bill, did you ever see a potato grader?"

The young man shook his head. "It's a long trough, with different size holes. The smallest potatoes fall through first; medium-size ones drop out farther down the trough, and the biggest go all the way. If you're bigger and better than the others, you'll make it all the way—just like the premium potatoes. It's up to you."

Bill accepted this curious comparison silently, although tears filled his eyes. (*That* made him angry, too!) But the talk triggered something inside. He began working harder at everything he did: he practiced oboe more, worked harder at his tennis game; he studied more diligently, and slowly he grew into a bigger potato! The ambition to be first class and the drive to work hard enough to make it is inside you.

Many people think luck makes one a better musician, a better student—even a better PR man. Don't you believe it. It's working at what you do, and working hard. That helps make the luck happen.

4. *Objective thinking.* All we think, say and do reflects our own framework of experience. But the clear thinker scrapes away his personal prejudices, his own persuasions, and tries to consider every problem and project objectively. *What are the facts?* What you feel is less important than what actually *is.*

5.   *Flexible attitude.* This is a two-sided coin: the other side is an *open mind.* One is as important as the other, and they complement each other. How many ways are there to do something? If there's just *your* way, you're in trouble, whether it's hitting a ball or taking an exam. What's right for you is important, but it's not the *only* right method or means. The other fellow might have a sounder system. Listen, with an open mind, and you may learn. Then be flexible in your actions or means.

6.   *Interest in service.* Public relations activity invokes a high sense of service: the common denominator of most activity is *others*—special groups, particular publics. Your role is a catalyst of a kind; you create things, make things happen, but you personally are secondary to results or conclusions. Whenever a spotlight shines, it may be focused on your company or client—but not you. Your own sense of satisfaction for a job well done is far more meaningful than the glare of the spotlight—*if* you're serious about a career in PR.

7.   *Friendliness.* "Easy with others" is one expert's definition. Are you genuinely interested in other people? Do you care about their problems? An amicable attitude toward the world around you is an asset for public relations work; but there's a definite line *before* the back-slapping, good-time-Charley role. You must know the difference. Others do.

8.   *Ability to do a large variety of tasks.* Every area of public relations work, whether in an agency or within a company, requires a flexibility of mind and capability to do many things. You must be able to drop one task and pick up another smoothly without lost motion or resentment. The

nature of PR demands a capacity to think and do more than one thing at a time. You'll often have several jobs going at the same time—photography to schedule, an interview to arrange, copy to be edited, a report to get out. You must be able to evaluate which takes precedence and do that first. You must be able to handle each job with equanimity—professionally, quickly, smoothly. It's not always easy!

9. *Lack of self-consciousness.* Public relations work involves considerable contact and exchange with all kinds of people—clients, media, suppliers and your own cohorts. Being self-aware is one thing; self-conscious is quite another. If you're embarrassed, shy or ill-at-ease with others, you'll be miserable in most PR jobs. To be self-*aware*, on the other hand, means self-knowledge, self-analysis and healthy introspection. The ability to examine your own strengths and weaknesses can be cultivated through discipline. Hard? Indeed! Diogenes Laertius in 200 A.D. remarked, "When Thales was asked what was difficult, he said, 'To know one's self.' And what was easy, 'To advise another.' "

10. *Ability to control tension.* This is an area that requires real self-awareness. Public relations is a fast-paced, demanding, often difficult field. People often make unreasonable demands and pressure is considerable. Every day is different, although many mechanics and situations are similar. Your work will be criticized, your copy edited; if you're sensitive to pressures, moods and an erratic schedule, you won't function well under the tensions that are part of everyday living in PR. To many, these tensions are part of the game—exciting, challenging and interesting. Be accurate with yourself—a calm exterior and churning insides create havoc. Maybe ulcers.

There are other factors that point toward a successful career in public relations. One is the ability to learn about anything, if you're really interested. Aldous Huxley says it well:

"Every man who knows how to read has it in his power to

magnify himself, to multiply the ways in which he exists, to make his life full, significant and interesting."

To be a good public relations practitioner requires a great many qualities, abilities and interests. It takes work and a genuine desire to be better than just average. This is an age of abbreviations and initials; to know your way in and out of the front page of a newspaper, you must know an entire series of initials. Here's another set, strictly for PR: TDK. Defined, it's simply: *Technical skills/ Dedication/ Knowledge* of the business. A steady supply of TDK will help insure your success!

—*Technical skills.* First of all, you must type. This is one skill you must learn to expedite your job. You should be able to write; this too is something you can learn. Clear, succinct, logical writing reflects an orderly mind, and does not preclude creativity.

—*Dedication.* You should like what you do. This seemingly obvious statement is often *not* the case. Yet more time, more actual hours are expended in work than any other given activity. When you choose a vocation you enjoy, it's a challenge to devote time and interest to your work. One PR executive in agency work becomes excited as a boy whenever a new account is in the offing; he spends time researching the company, considers all the problem areas and spends hours on possible resolutions of these problems. He also happens to be president of one of the big ten PR agencies! Phil Klarnet, president of Edward Gottlieb & Associates, is a dedicated and enthusiastic champion of PR and publicity. At the Publicity Club of New York's Twenty-fifth Anniversary Dinner he was the key speaker and left these typical thoughts with his audience: "Publicity is one of the vital forces in the world today. Modern business enterprise recognizes the value of publicity to the point where it is an essential part of the marketing operations of virtually every corporation dealing with the consumer. . . . Creative, exciting—you can make it what you like, and your satisfactions are there in print and on the air as well as the bank teller's window. Businesslike methods, high ethical standards . . . make publicity a great business to be in. With them, you're bound to be proud of what you're doing. And that pride will reflect itself in your attitude toward an editor, the client you serve, the men and women you work with. Pride in publicity . . . is up to you."

—*Knowledge of the business.* This may be the hardest to acquire. The more you learn about your company or client, the better equipped you'll be to do an above-average job. If you work for General Motors, every moment you spend learning everything possible about cars is vital; spend *more* time learning about safety, foreign car manufacturing, travel. No matter what your actual business is, read all you can about it, then read more about peripheral businesses.

What the pros look for. A few years ago 165 public relations executives were polled for their opinions on important qualities desired in a PR person; these executives were responsible for hiring and firing PR people in companies, counseling firms, government, non-profit and association jobs. The results of thier survey appeared in the *Public Relations Journal* and are repeated here. Listed in the order of importance, the desired qualities include:

1. Ability to think
2. Judgment
3. Ability to write
4. Pleasant personality
5. Maturity
6. Ability to speak
7. Good appearance
8. Wide interests
9. Broad, liberal arts background

These are the qualities that public relations bosses look for in a new applicant. Some of these qualities he can assess after talking with you briefly; other qualities—integrity, curiosity, senstivity, creativity—reveal themselves only through association or, very often, in psychological tests. Some companies require testing prior to hiring. Paul Zucker, executive vice-president of Ruder and Finn, one of the nation's largest public relations firms, says unequivocally, "Don't be afraid of taking psychological tests. Every individual in our organization has been tested. The experience has done us good. For example, I learned about myself that I have a tendency to be hard or negative on ideas that aren't my own . . . When you've taken the test, don't be ashamed to discuss the results with the interviewer. That's his job—to tell you what your strengths and limitations are.

"You can get tests like this through your local university's psychology department or even, in some cities, at the YMCA."

Testing can be an invaluable aid to you, to know both your own shortcomings and positives more clearly. When you have the opportunity to take any of the modern battery of psychological tests available today, do so. You'll learn much about yourself and what areas need shoring up.

How do you rate? Just how accurate are you when you look in the mirror? Psychologists claim the mirrored reflection is a composite of half what we expect to see, one-quarter what we actually view, and the last quarter? What we would like to see!

Here's a simple, explicit checklist for you to measure your own self-awareness and your ability to evaluate yourself honestly, if not accurately. Give yourself a score of from 1 to 10 on each of the following checkpoints. A score of 10 is the highest count for each item. Think about each point, but don't ponder.

TEST YOUR PUBLIC RELATIONS QUOTIENT

Administrative ability .... ⎯⎯⎯
Creative thinker .... ⎯⎯⎯
Diplomatic .... ⎯⎯⎯
Extrovert type .... ⎯⎯⎯
Good on detail .... ⎯⎯⎯
Instinct and intuition .... ⎯⎯⎯
Leadership .... ⎯⎯⎯
Appearance .... ⎯⎯⎯
Organizer and planner .... ⎯⎯⎯
Public speaker .... ⎯⎯⎯
Sales ability .... ⎯⎯⎯
Sound judgment .... ⎯⎯⎯
Writing ability .... ⎯⎯⎯

Total your score, and check your results with what PR experts say about it.

—*100 or more.* You must be kidding! Better go back and recheck your scoring. A positive opinion of yourself is important, but nobody *that* effective has been around for several centuries. Review each point, then rescore yourself.

—*80 to 100.* You've chosen the right field—you can succeed in public relations! You're sufficiently self-aware to recognize your strong points, as well as weak areas. Review each attribute—plus and minus—and decide where you can strengthen your profile. Obviously, many of the qualities which contribute to an effective public relations career parallel those which characterize an effective, productive human being. Keep working!

—*70 to 80.* Chances are you'll reach the top; your realistic self-awareness is a sound asset; keep abreast of all around you—events, people, situations, developments; you can become a crack PR person.

—*60 to 70.* You can still climb to impressive heights in

public relations, but you'll have to invest more of yourself in your business than you've been willing to give so far. Your score indicates definite strength in certain aspects. Where you fall down is where you must begin to bolster immediately. Your midway score also indicates you might dislike certain categories, such as detail. But if necessary, you *can* do it. Examine your individual scorings, and realistically evaluate how accurate your answers were. Review your scores again, and get to work!

—*50 to 60.* Either your self-evaluation standards are highly inaccurate, or you're attracted to public relations for all the wrong reasons. The activity is stimulating, challenging and often satisfying; but PR work *is* work. Test your PR Quotient again if you're serious; if your total remains at this low level, and you're *still* interested in PR—good! There's always room if you have the drive to direct your ambitions and energies. Good luck!

—*50 or less.* There's a whole wide world of activity out there—happily, for you, removed from public relations! Unless you're totally misguided about yourself, you would fare better in another business or profession. Perhaps you skimmed the book too rapidly and don't understand what PR is all about. Try it again, but read it this time. Then check your PR Quotient once more; if you still score under 50, the field of public relations is not for you.

Now you know the score; what are you going to do about it? The next chapter tells you how to go about reserving room at the top.

15 Reserve Room at the Top

What you wear may make a difference in your entree and progress in the field of public relations. The fashion now and for years to come, for both young men and girls, is a cap and gown! College training and a degree are increasingly important in PR. The primary reason for a good, solid educational background is that you'll be dealing with problems and situations that demand a mind trained to evaluate.

Recently, a study was made by Robert W. Miller of the American University of corporate executive attitudes toward public relations. One observation from this study reflects top management's thinking about PR men:

"In many cases, the chief executive officer . . . feels that, too often, the individual's background and training are not as broad as they should be for the work. The main criticism is that the public relations man is skilled in writing and in publicity-getting techniques and mechanics, but that he is not as useful to the firm as he should be, because he lacks an understanding of the over-all economic picture and of the local corporate picture."

This is the consensus of 250 corporation chairmen and

presidents of major businesses in this country. The single most effective way to increase your knowledge now is through good academic training.

Executives in PR share this opinion on the importance of an education. John F. Budd, Jr., a vice-president of Carl Byoir & Associates, Inc., another of the country's large public relations firms, says in the *PR Reporter* (June 6, 1966):

"A college degree is becoming a prerequisite for PR, although perhaps not for publicity writing; but remember that publicity is only one of the many tools, or techniques, of PR. There are many instances, for example, where a community's attitude toward a company must be analyzed perceptively. Such a function, properly a PR man's function, wouldn't involve a line of publicity copy. Instead, some familiarity with sociology and psychology, and an ability to assay the political environment, would be of far more practical value than writing."

John Hill says in his book *The Making of a Public Relations Man*, "Competence in public relations requires a combination of many qualities. I have mentioned integrity and judgment. I would also emphasize education and training. Four years of college have become virtually mandatory. *The college degree is important in getting a job, but more telling are the dimensions of the learning the diploma represents.*"

This perspective was repeated by Edward Bernays during a Speakerphone interview between him and students at Pace College in New York. Mr. Bernays told the young people:

"Actually, in public relations your effectiveness depends fundamentally on your knowledge of the society—sociology, social psychology. It is dependent upon your understanding of people and their motivations and attitudes. It is dependent on your creative imagination in appraising, interpreting a situation and implementing action based on your interpretation. To do this you need a good academic background of sociology, social psychology, public opinion. You need ability to act professionally—that is, to apply your art to science—to act creatively in bringing about new juxtapositions of people and events so that attitudes and actions may be changed."

There should be little question in your mind about the importance of a good liberal college education. If it's impossible for you to continue your schooling, you still can continue working on the learning process—this should be a lifetime avocation. And you can be a successful, productive and effective public relations person without a degree, of course, but it will be harder for you. The mental demands and intellectual disciplines gained from higher education make every effort you put toward that education well worth the investment, no matter how difficult it may be for you.

What about the courses? Leaders in the field recommend solid liberal arts training. Courses in economics, sociology, psychology, English, political sciences, history and literature are important. Your guidance counselor can advise you on a sound, comprehensive course of study in the humanities.

What about actual courses in public relations and related areas? Experts are sharply divided on the value of academic PR training. Some eschew college public relations training completely; others believe the exposure provides some insight into the field, but the practical value is minimal.

"I'm against all training schools," avows Dr. Paul A. Wagner, Director of Education at Hill and Knowlton. "Training schools for art, drama, or public relations. But a general liberal education for PR? It's imperative," says the director.

"A liberal education gives you a feeling for the field. You need that, of course. You learn to be sensitive to semantics, and develop a heart for these matters. Whatever field of knowledge you follow in school will be useful to you. The *discipline* you learn from any area of study—law, sociology, or psychology—gives you a better awareness of that field. This, in turn, gives you a respect for it—and from respect you develop a self-imposed discipline. That's the important thing."

Dr. Wagner, a big, vibrant man with a contagious enthusiasm, works in a large, bright office that resembles a professor's study—books, papers and manuals are stacked carefully in all available space; a Picasso "blue period" print leans against a chair, waiting to be hung.

"Basically, I'm a communicator," he smiled. "When I was teaching, I was a communicator; working on a news magazine also was communicating. I hold a union card as a screen director—when I produce a film, that's communicating.

"In public relations, our work is communication." He paused. "Most communicators are agents of change. By that, I mean that *real* communicators hope to create a better humanity. Does that sound far-reaching? Well, the ethical PR man is an agent of change; his job is communicating new ideas, advancements and services to people. Change is going on constantly, of course. As an agent of change, you're a catalyst in communication. You help make things happen."

Dr. Wagner swung away from his work-piled desk and looked out at the Manhattan skyline from his Forty-second Street office window.

"I think you'll find a shift toward highly educated generalists in public relations. These will be the problem-solvers of tomorrow. For example, suppose one of your clients happens to be a beer company that's interested in sponsoring a jazz festival—something like Newport. What do you advise them? You've got to know a lot about ethnic groups, about sociology. What are the cultural aspects of such an event? You've got to know how kids think, too—how they'd react." Dr. Wagner edged forward on his chair, exuding eagerness as he talked. "You see? Narrowness is a defect. You'll have to know things far beyond any special confines. The more you

know, the better off you'll be. The better educated a generalist you are, the better a PR person you'll be."

Another executive in the agency business, Charles Lipton,
vice-president of Ruder & Finn, feels strongly about public
relations training in school.

"A graduate degree in PR is fine. Chances are, if he's a
grad student, he's also working in some allied field or has
had actual working experience. But the undergrad program
in public relations?" The dynamic young executive shook his
head. "The great lack in academic PR is you don't learn
enough about business. Yet business supports public relations."

Mr. Lipton has been directly involved with student recruitment programs during the past few years. Although the
actual recruitment of college students for PR agency work
has barely started in comparison to other industries, there is
enough progress to indicate some reaction from the professionals:

"We've had some great kids come through, but they're
more the exception. Our strongest criticism of most college
kids, I believe, is that they lack initiative. There's a tremendous opportunity today for kids willing to do a little home-
work. Most couldn't care less. In today's job market, kids
don't have to worry about finding a job. But this won't last,
and when it's tighter, it's the young people with initiative
who'll make it.

What about special interests? If you're drawn to special
areas—science, food, politics and government—there are
courses which will be particularly helpful to you. To get into
science public relations, for example, you should have a
sound academic background in chemistry, math, biology,
astronomy, physics. The social sciences are extremely important—psychology, sociology, history, anthropology.

Food publicists should have home economics training

and, preferably, a degree. The burgeoning areas of governmental agency and political public relations will require knowledge of the social sciences, economics, history and political science—to name only a few. Again, your counselor or advisor can guide you toward the most useful and broad-based curriculum for your interests and goals.

Extra credits. Public relations experts polled for their views on whether or not extra-curricular activity is important responded with a resounding "yes!" You started your life work in high school, both academically and in organization activity. Your campus life also is a powerful character builder—whether you're working in a lab, waiting tables, selling in a store or at football practice. These activities are considered by your future employers; they indicate a lot about you, your interests and abilities.

Campus activities rated as significant for what they contribute to an eventual career in public relations include work on school publications, both the newspaper and yearbook. Editorial staff work is particularly noteworthy. Campus organizations such as student government, clubs, fraternities and sororities all contribute to the learning-about-others process. Athletics rank importantly, for the physical discipline they demand. Student teaching is a splendid real-life course in communications. All the activity you can swing will be to your advantage. Notice that "swing"—really take part in and contribute to the activity's development. Just being a joiner is shallow skimming and indicates a negative or minus side of character.

School's out—what's next? Cracking the job market is next on the agenda, and there may be times you'll wish you were back conjugating verbs. Experience or the lack of it can be a problem. Many public relations departments and agencies require media experience for their personnel. The rigors of working on a newspaper help you learn the disciplines of good writing, objectivity and speed.

Teaching is a helpful beginning for the public relations generalist of tomorrow. You'll learn basic communication— the effectiveness and "art of plain talk." The sales training programs of major companies will give you an insight into marketing and sales, another plus in the PR world.

To move directly into public relations from school is difficult, but not impossible. Review the chapter on the four major working areas of PR; decide which category appeals to you most and which one your abilities would be best suited for.

If it's an agency, you'll do best to get a media job for at least one year; you'll progress faster with the experience. A corporate PR job may be easier to break into directly, such as an assistant's job, perhaps working on a company house organ. The association and non-profit fields often prefer some work experience, but again you might merit an apprentice job, based on a good academic record.

The important thing is that any solid working experience will serve you well for public relations; just don't get discouraged; define your goal, then keep working at it. You'll make it!

About that reservation for "Room at the Top." You'll have to make your own. Public relations offers no sinecure for the future. There's no shingle to hang, no universally recognized professional stature. One of the greatest progressive steps toward "official" recognition of the PR practitioner is the accreditation program of the Public Relations Society of America. (See Chapter 3.)

PRSA is the most influential of the associations of public relations practitioners; accreditation by this group is earned upon merit and service and may serve to strengthen the professional status of the entire field. The power of PRSA is considerable within its own membership. For example, the organization voted to censure Chicago PR man Julius Klein in September 23, 1963. Klein was cited for his lobbying activities on behalf of the West German government. The New York *Post* reported: "Ward B. Stevenson, then president of the Society, sent out a notice to all members stating that the Board of Directors had voted to censure Klein for 'violation of paragraphs 1 and 13 of the society's Code of Professional Standards for the Practice of Public Relations.'"

This meant that among his peers Julius Klein was then *persona non grata*. A parallel would be a lawyer disbarred from practice by the Bar Association.

Other Public Relations organizations. Several special interest groups involved in public relations activity have formed their own associations. These include such groups as The Agricultural Relations Council, the American College Public Relations Association, Bank Public Relations and Marketing Association, Chemical Public Relations Association, Library Public Relations Council, Religious Public Relations—just to note a few.

Brave new world. Before 1987 this country will undergo impressive upheavals in life as we know it, according to sociologists. By 1980, for example, the surge toward centralization will be marked; more than 250 million people will be clustered around the few great cities of America. John Hill (*PR Journal*, September 1965) predicts, "There will be mounting problems of social welfare, of schools, of housing, of transportation and much else, most of which will be federal government financed . . . it surely will create staggering public relations problems for private industry."

Other areas which will be of concern to public relations people, according to Mr. Hill, include education, supplying the wants of an increased population, a communication and transportation "explosion," automation and the tremendous increase in shareholders of corporate stock. Each area will present new problems in communications and comprehension, and these problems will demand solution.

Mr. Hill further predicts, "Above all, public relations for

business will develop its power of communications, reaching into the minds and hearts and emotions of people to gain their understanding, good will and support, to the extent deserved."

Are you ready for tomorrow? Consider this list carefully; sage counselors of today's world suggest each of these areas will require the knowledge, understanding and ability to cope with each effectively—all part of the PR job of tomorrow:

—*Individual behavior.* How people are motivated, and why; lucid self-knowledge and clear insight into the behavior of others.

—*Group behavior.* How groups are formed, why, and what influences them.

—*Communication process.* Depth knowledge of mass media; their role and limitations in opinion formation and cultivation. New ideas—their birth, nurture and development.

—*Government—its structure and functioning.* How government agencies work; what happens to public issues.

—*Business system.* The force and direction of tomorrow's business will have a vital effect on our own society and that of the world.

—*Science—"where the action is."* Comprehension of the wondrous unknowns will unlock incredible new worlds.

Each of these fields of knowledge requires your attention, long before 1987. The more you learn about each, the more inquisitive you'll become. The capaciousness of the knowledge process may surprise even you!

Computer public relations. A scientist from a California university predicts that a computer may replace the PR man in the future. The computer will turn out pristine copy—proper grammar, spelling, punctuation—and "eliminate *irrevelant* material," according to the UPI story by Paul Jeschke with an August 21 dateline from San Francisco.

Obviously no computer prepared this copy, which whizzed along today's teletype machine complete with misspelling.

Nor will a computer replace tomorrow's PR man—as long as the public relations man or woman takes his proper place with the *thinking* individuals of the world. Thinking is the first requisite for communication, and effective communicators will be in greater demand than ever tomorrow.

There's a remarkable "brave new world" waiting for you in the ranks of public relations; if you like what you know about it, go claim that world. You'll enjoy it!

Sources of Further Information

Accredited colleges and universities offering degrees and courses in public relations. For detailed information, write directly to the school. This listing was compiled in 1967 by the Public Relations Society of America.

I. SCHOOLS OFFERING DEGREES IN PUBLIC RELATIONS

MASTER'S DEGREE

DISTRICT OF COLUMBIA
The American University, Department of Journalism, Public Relations and Broadcasting

GEORGIA
University of Georgia, School of Journalism, Athens

MASSACHUSETTS
Boston University, School of Public Communication, Boston

MICHIGAN
Michigan State University, College of Communication Arts, East Lansing

NEW YORK
Pace College, Graduate School of Business Administration, New York City

Syracuse University, School of Journalism, Syracuse

BACHELOR'S DEGREE

CALIFORNIA
San Jose State College, Department of Journalism and Advertising, San Jose

University of Southern California, School of Journalism, University Park, Los Angeles

GEORGIA
University of Georgia, School of Journalism, Athens

MASSACHUSETTS
Boston University, School of Public Communication, Boston

NEW YORK
Syracuse University, School of Journalism, Syracuse

Utica College of Syracuse University, Division of Business Administration, Utica

II. SCHOOLS REPORTING SPECIAL SEQUENCES IN PUBLIC RELATIONS

GRADUATE LEVEL

DISTRICT OF COLUMBIA
The American University, School of Business Administration.

CONNECTICUT
Fairfield University, Graduate School of Corporate and Political Communication, Fairfield

INDIANA
Ball State University, Department of Journalism, Muncie

IOWA
University of Iowa, School of Journalism, Iowa City

MINNESOTA
University of Minnesota, School of Journalism and Mass Communication, Minneapolis

NEW YORK
City College of the City University of New York, School of Business and Public Administration, New York City

OHIO
Ohio State University, School of Journalism, Columbus
Ohio University, School of Journalism, Athens

OKLAHOMA
University of Oklahoma, School of Journalism, Norman

OREGON
University of Oregon, School of Journalism, Eugene

WEST VIRGINIA
West Virginia University, School of Journalism, Morgantown

WISCONSIN
University of Wisconsin, School of Journalism, Madison

UNDERGRADUATE LEVEL

DISTRICT OF COLUMBIA
The American University, Department of Journalism, Public Relations and Broadcasting

CALIFORNIA
Fresno State College, School of Professional Studies, Fresno

FLORIDA
Florida State University, School of Business, Tallahassee

INDIANA
Ball State University, Department of Journalism, Muncie

IDAHO
Idaho State University, Department of Journalism, Pocatello

IOWA
University of Iowa, School of Journalism, Iowa City

KANSAS
Washburn University of Topeka, School of Business, Topeka

MARYLAND
University of Maryland, College of Business and Public Administration, College Park

MINNESOTA
University of Minnesota, School of Journalism and Mass Communication, Minneapolis

MISSISSIPPI
University of Southern Mississippi, Department of Communication, Hattiesburg

NEBRASKA
University of Omaha, School of Journalism, Omaha

NEW JERSEY
Rutgers University, School of Journalism, New Brunswick

NEW MEXICO
New Mexico State University, Department of Journalism and Mass Communication, Las Cruces

NEW YORK
City College of the City University of New York, School of Business and Public Administration, New York City

OHIO
Bowling Green State University, School of Journalism, Bowling Green

Kent State University, School of Journalism, Kent

Ohio State University, School of Journalism, Columbus

Ohio University, School of Journalism, Athens

OKLAHOMA
Oklahoma State University, School of Journalism, Stillwater
University of Oklahoma, School of Journalism, Norman

PENNSYLVANIA
Duquesne University, School of Journalism, Pittsburgh

TEXAS
Baylor University, College of Arts and Sciences, Waco
University of Houston, Department of Management and Business Administration, Houston
Southern Methodist University, Department of Journalism, Dallas
University of Texas, Department of Journalism, Austin

WEST VIRGINIA
West Virginia University, School of Journalism, Morgantown

WISCONSIN
University of Wisconsin, School of Journalism, Madison

III. SCHOOLS REPORTING TWO OR MORE COURSES IN PUBLIC RELATIONS

GRADUATE LEVEL

ARIZONA
Arizona State University, Marketing Department—College of Business, Tempe

FLORIDA
University of Florida, School of Journalism and Communications, Gainesville

ILLINOIS
Northern Illinois University, Journalism Department, DeKalb

KANSAS
University of Kansas, School of Journalism, Lawrence

MASSACHUSETTS
Emerson College, Department of Broadcasting, Boston

MISSISSIPPI
University of Mississippi, School of Journalism, University

MISSOURI
Central Missouri State College, Speech Department, Warrensburg

NEVADA
University of Nevada, Department of Journalism, Reno

OHIO
Bowling Green State University, Graduate School of Business Administration, Bowling Green

PENNSYLVANIA
Pennsylvania State University, School of Journalism, University Park
Temple University, School of Communications, Philadelphia

SOUTH DAKOTA
South Dakota State University, School of Journalism, Brookings

UNDERGRADUATE LEVEL

ALABAMA
Samford University, School of Journalism, Birmingham

ARIZONA
Arizona State University, Mass Communications Department—College of Liberal Arts, Tempe

CALIFORNIA
California State College at Fullerton, Department of Communications, Fullerton
California State College, School of Government, Los Angeles
California State Polytechnic College, Department of Technical Journalism, San Luis Obispo
San Diego State College, School of Journalism, San Diego
San Francisco State College, Department of Marketing, San Francisco

COLORADO
Colorado State University, Tech-

nical Journalism Division, Fort Collins
Southern Colorado State College, Department of Journalism, Pueblo

DISTRICT OF COLUMBIA
George Washington University, Department of Journalism

FLORIDA
University of Florida, School of Journalism and Communications, Gainesville

IDAHO
University of Idaho, School of Journalism, Moscow

ILLINOIS
Illinois Institute of Technology, Department of Business and Economics, Chicago
Northern Illinois University, Journalism Department, DeKalb
Southern Illinois University,

School of Communication, Carbondale

INDIANA
Indiana University, Department of Journalism, Bloomington

IOWA
Drake University, Journalism Department, Des Moines

KANSAS
University of Kansas, School of Journalism, Lawrence

LOUISIANA
Loyola University, Journalism Department, New Orleans

MASSACHUSETTS
Emerson College, Department of Broadcasting, Boston

MICHIGAN
Hillsdale College, Department of Economics, Hillsdale
Michigan State University, College of Communication Arts, East Lansing

MISSISSIPPI
University of Mississippi, School of Journalism, University
Mississippi State College for Women, Department of Journalism, Columbus

MISSOURI
Central Missouri State College, Speech Department, Warrensburg

NEBRASKA
Creighton University, School of Journalism, Omaha

NEVADA
University of Nevada, Department of Journalism, Reno

NEW HAMPSHIRE
Manchester Institute of Arts and Sciences, Adult Study Program, Manchester*

NEW YORK
Cornell University, School of Industrial and Labor Relations and Agricultural College, Ithaca
New School for Social Research, School of Business, New York City*

OHIO
University of Toledo, College of Education and Division of Journalism Studies, Toledo
Youngstown University, Department of Business Organization, Youngstown

OKLAHOMA
Northeastern State University, Department of Communication, Tahlequah

OREGON
University of Oregon, School of Journalism, Eugene

PENNSYLVANIA
Pennsylvania State University, School of Journalism, University Park

SOUTH DAKOTA
University of South Dakota, School of Journalism, Vermillion
South Dakota State University, School of Journalism, Brookings

VIRGINIA
Bridgewater College, Department of Business and Economics, Bridgewater

WEST VIRGINIA
Bethany College, School of Journalism, Bethany

* Non-credit

IV. SCHOOLS REPORTING AT LEAST ONE COURSE IN PUBLIC RELATIONS

ALASKA
University of Alaska, Department of Journalism, College

ARKANSAS
University of Arkansas, Department of Journalism, Fayetteville

CALIFORNIA
Bakersfield College, Department of Journalism, Bakersfield
California State College at Long Beach, School of Journalism, Long Beach
California State College at Los Angeles, School of Business and Economics, Los Angeles
University of California at Los Angeles, Department of Journalism, Los Angeles
Chico State College, Language Arts Department, Chico
University of the Pacific, Department of Economics and Business Administration, Stockton
University of Redlands, Department of Journalism, Redlands
San Fernando Valley State College, Journalism and Broadcasting Department, Northridge
Woodbury College, Department of Journalism, Los Angeles

COLORADO
Adams State College, School of Education, Alamosa
University of Colorado, School of Journalism, Boulder
University of Denver, School of Business Administration, Denver
Fort Lewis College, Division of Business and Economics, Durango

CONNECTICUT
University of Bridgeport, Journalism Department, Bridgeport
University of Connecticut, School of Business Administration, Storrs

FLORIDA
University of Miami, School of Business Administration, Coral Gables

GEORGIA
Albany State College, Department of English, Albany

ILLINOIS
Bradley University, Journalism Department, Peoria
University of Illinois, Department of Advertising, Urbana
Principia College, Department of Economics and Business Administration, Elsah
Roosevelt University, College of Business Administration, Chicago

IOWA
Clarke College, School of Journalism, Dubuque

KANSAS
Baker University, School of Jouralism, Baldwin
Kansas State University, College of Arts and Sciences, Manhattan

KENTUCKY
University of Kentucky, Department of Journalism, Lexington
Morehead State University, Division of Communications, Morehead
Western Kentucky University,

Bowling Green College of Commerce, Bowling Green

LOUISIANA
Louisiana State University, School of Business Administration, Baton Rouge
Northwestern State College, Department of Languages, Natchitoches
Tulane University, University College, New Orleans

MASSACHUSETTS
American International College (Non-departmental) Springfield
Babson Institute, Distribution Division, Babson Park

MICHIGAN
Central Michigan University, Department of Journalism, Mt. Pleasant
University of Michigan, School of Journalism, Ann Arbor
Wayne State University, Department of Marketing, Detroit

MINNESOTA
College of St. Catherine, Department of Journalism, St. Paul
University of Minnesota at Duluth, Department of English, Duluth
Winona State College, Division of Language and Literature, Winona

MISSOURI
University of Missouri, School of Journalism, Columbia
Washington University, Evening Division, St. Louis*

NEBRASKA
University of Nebraska, School of Journalism, Lincoln

NEW JERSEY
Fairleigh Dickinson University, College of Business Administration, Rutherford

NEW MEXICO
Eastern New Mexico University, Department of Journalism, Portales

NEW YORK
Columbia University, School of General Studies, New York City
Cornell University, Graduate School of Business and Public Administration, Ithaca
Fordham University, Thomas More College for Women, New York City
Long Island University, Department of Journalism, Brooklyn
New York City Community College, Department of Marketing, Brooklyn, New York
New York University, Journalism Department, New York City
Queens College of the City University of New York, School of General Studies—Adult Education, Flushing*

OHIO
University of Akron, College of Business Administration, Akron
Cleveland State University, Marketing Department, Cleveland
College of Steubenville, Department of Communications, Steubenville
Dyke College, College of Business Administration, Cleveland

OKLAHOMA
Phillips University, School of Business Administration, Enid

Non-credit   *Non-credit*

University of Tulsa, Journalism Department, Tulsa

OREGON
Pacific University, Department of Journalism, Forest Grove
Portland State College, School of Business, Portland

RHODE ISLAND
University of Rhode Island, Department of Journalism, Kingston

SOUTH CAROLINA
Newberry College, School of Economics and Business Administration, Newberry

TENNESSEE
University of Chattanooga, School of Business Administration, Chattanooga
Memphis State University, Department of Journalism, Memphis

TEXAS
Arlington State College, Department of English, Arlington
Houston Baptist College, Division of Business and Economics, Houston
Mary Hardin-Baylor College, School of Business, Belton
North Texas State University, Department of Journalism, Denton
St. Edward's University, Division of Business Administration, Austin

Sul Ross State College, School of Journalism, Alpine
University of Texas at El Paso, Department of Mass Communication, El Paso
Texas A & M University, Department of Journalism, College Station
Texas Christian University, Department of Journalism and School of Business, Fort Worth
Texas Technological College, Department of Journalism, Lubbock
Trinity University, School of Journalism, San Antonio

UTAH
Brigham Young University, Department of Communications, Provo
University of Utah, Department of Journalism, Ogden
Weber State College, School of Journalism, Fairmont

WEST VIRGINIA
Fairmont State College, Department of Journalism, Fairmont
Marshall University, Journalism Department, Huntington

WISCONSIN
University of Wisconsin, Department of Journalism, Milwaukee
Wisconsin State University, Department of Journalism, Oshkosh
Wisconsin State University, Department of Journalism, Superior

BIBLIOGRAPHY

Bernays, Edward L., *Public Relations*, University of Oklahoma Press, 1952

Hill, John W., *The Making of a Public Relations Man*, David McKay Co., 1963

Stein, M. L., *Your Career in Journalism*, Julian Messner, 1965

Cutlip, Scott M. and Center, Allen H., *Effective Public Relations*, Second Edition, Prentice-Hall, 1958

Hiebert, Ray, *Courtier to A Crowd*, Iowa State University Press, 1966

Flesch, Rudolf, *How to be Brief*, Harper & Row, 1962

Lesley, Philip, *Public Relations Handbook*, Prentice-Hall, 1962

Harlow, Rex F. and Black, Marvin M., *Practical Public Relations*, Revised Ed., Harper & Bros., 1952

Baus, Herbert M., *Publicity in Action*, Harper & Bros., 1954

Whyte, William H., *Is Anybody Listening?*, Simon & Schuster, 1952

INDEX